# Madrid

Spain

**EVERYMAN**
CITY GUIDES

**EVERYMAN CITY GUIDES**
Copyright © 1998 David
Campbell Publishers, London

ISBN 1-85715-828-8

*First published February 1998*

Originally published in
France by Nouveaux Loisirs,
a subsidiary of Gallimard,
Paris 1997, and in Italy by
Touring Editore, Srl.,
Milano 1997.
Copyright © 1997
Nouveaux Loisirs,
Touring Editore, Srl.

**SERIES EDITORS**
EDITORIAL MANAGER:
Seymourina Cruse
MADRID EDITION: Vincent de
Lapomarède, Caroline Cuny
and David Beytelmann
**GRAPHICS**
Élizabeth Cohat, Yann Le Duc
LAYOUT: Olivier Lauga, Yann
Le Duc
MINI-MAPS, AIRPORT MAPS:
Kristoff Chemineau
MADRID MAPS:
Édigraphie
STREET MAPS:
Touring Club Italiano
**PRODUCTION**
Catherine Bourrabier

Translated by Laura Ward
Edited and typeset by Book
Creation Services, London

Printed in Italy by
Editoriale Libraria

Authors
**MADRID**
## Things you need to know:
Pilar Careaga (1)
Author of travel guides on CD-Rom, Pilar
Careaga spent her teenage years guiding
visitors around the Prado museum.

## Where to stay and where to eat: Victor de la Serna (2)
Victor de la Serna has written about food
for the Spanish newspapers *El País*, *Diario 16*
and *El Mundo*. He was the Spanish
correspondent for the London magazine
*Decanter* and a columnist for the Spanish
*Sibarita* magazine. He is now joint editor of
the daily *El Mundo*.

## After dark: Jaime Iglesias (3)
Jaime Iglesias trained as a lawyer and
journalist and is now a publicity director.
He has been among Madrid's night-owls for
many years.

## What to see:
Mariano Navarro (4)
Consultant to the Spanish TV program
*Trazos e Imágenes*, exhibition curator, editor
of books for bibliophiles and writer of
supplements on Velázquez, Goya and
Gauguin for *El País Semanal*, Mariano
Navarro is currently arranging Madrid's
latest exhibitions of 20th-century art.

## Further afield:
Consuelo Álvarez de Miranda (5)
Art historian and expert on Baroque
architecture, Consuelo Álvarez de Miranda
has taught in various schools, edited the six-
volume *Historia del arte hispánico* (1976–
1980) and was joint author of the guide
*Madrid práctico – Todo Madrid* (1995).

## Where to shop:
Paloma Sarasúa (6)
Author, journalist and sociologist, Pilar
Sarasúa has just published *Trabaja, mujer,
trabaja* for Acento Editorial, an essay on
women's work in modern-day society. She
was also joint author of the guide *Madrid
práctico – Todo Madrid* (1993).

---

*Note from the publisher:
To keep the price of this guide as low as
possible we decided on a common edition for
the UK and US, which has meant
American spelling.*

# Things you need to know ➥6

# Where to stay ➥16

# Where to eat ➥34

# After dark ➥66

# What to see ➥88

# Further afield ➥110

# Where to shop ➥124

# Maps ➥146

# How to use this guide

This guide is divided into eight separate sections: **Everything you need to know** (information on travel and living in Madrid); **Where to stay** (hotels); **Where to eat** (restaurants); **After dark** (going out); **What to see** (museums and monuments in the city); **Further afield** (places to visit around Madrid); **Where to shop** (store guide); **Maps** (street maps and plan of the subway.)

The **color** of the arrow box matches that of the corresponding dots on the mini-maps.

**In the area** gives you a feel for the location.

## In the area

Located north of Retiro Park, this part of developed into an upmarket shopping are

The **area** (or the subject on a thematic page) is shown just above the map. A map reference allows you to find places easily in the street map section.

## Serrano/Velázquez
D DI - FAI

48    19

## In the area

Located north of Retiro Park, this developed into an upmarket shop and luxury goods. It is here that the most prestigious commercial art galleries are located.

## Where to eat

■ Where to stay → 24
■ Where to shop → 130
138 → 140 → 144

### El Amparo (29)

Puigcerdá 8, 28001 ■ (91) 431 64 56 ■ (91) 575 54 91

■ Goya **Modern Spanish cuisine** ●●●● □ □ Mon.–Sat. 1.30–3.30pm,
9–11.30pm; closed Aug. 11–17

One of the finest and most innovative restaurants in Madrid, El Amparo was relaunched in 1993 when its arrival as culinary adviser of the Basque Counago, one of the most inspiring chefs to emerge from the Basque country. Several intimate dining areas laid out on different levels around a central interior courtyard Chillida could choose from the prawn and wild mushroom salad, the white truffle saffron could. The many-leaf turbot with spinach and a sauce and lobster could. The menu also includes a list of choice wines. Luis the cuisine could. The menu also sommeliers in Madrid, runs a well-stocked wine cellar of the best bottles of prestige and claret, some of the latest labels to cause a stir.

### La Paloma (30)

Jorge Juan 39, 28001 ■ (91) 576 86 92

■ Goya, Vergara **Creative gourmet cuisine** ●●●● □ □ Mon.–Sat.
1.30–4pm, 9–11.45pm; closed Easter week, Aug, public holidays

Segundo Alonso was head chef at El Amparo, but has now opened his own restaurant on the site of La Paloma. The decor is luxurious, and the service is impeccable, and the restaurant still the ame is well expensive, the service is impeccable, and decorated in the style it was previously, it has equally as undisputed master of cooking is an robust and appealing. An example of the stuffed with foie gras; baby spider crab and spinach and pigeon watercress coulis. He also creates some mouthwatering desserts.

### Teatriz (31)

Hermosilla 15, 28001 ■ (91) 577 53 79

■ Serrano **Italian cuisine** ●●● □ □ daily 1.30–4pm, 9pm–1am; closed in Aug.

A fashionable restaurant where many of the regulars are being squeezed out by crowds of newcomers who find this old theater not so lush for its superb cuisine but for its decor, designed by Philippe Starck in the early 1990s. Visit the exclusive Stars Bar, bathed in a bluish light, in the center of which stands a throne-like mountain of gold, marble and silver – you could be forgiven for thinking it's a nightclub.

### Not forgetting

■ **La Trainera** (32) Lagasca 60, 28001 ■ (91) 576 05 75 ●●●●
A rustic tasca serving up excellent seafood & fish, plus langoustines for meat-lovers, plus langoustines. ■ **El Pescador** (33) José Ortega y Gasset 75, 28006 ■ (91) 402 12 90 ●●●● A classy fish place with marble & dark wood, bottles of wine, and bread (brand name) for men. ■ **El Fogón** (33) Hotel Wellington, Villanueva 34, 28001 ■ (91) 575 44 00 A good hotel restaurant serving up classic Spanish dishes. Service is smooth.

The **area** (or the subject on a thematic page) is shown just above the map.

The Teatriz tabbern was designed by Phillippe Starck, the French architect and designer, who endeavours, great furniture importance to chapes and spaces.

### Not forgetting

■ **La Trainera (32**
A rustic tasca serving up
lovers, plus langoustines.

**Not forgetting** lists places we also recommend, but don't have space to cover in full here.

■ Goya, Vergara **Creative gourmet cuisine** ●
1.30–4pm, 9–11.45pm; closed Easter week, Au

Segundo Alonso was head chef at El Amp

**Key information** tells you what you need to know about each particular place: the nearest subway station; the price range, accepted means of payment, and the various services and facilities on offer.

The **opening page** of each section gives an index of its contents and some helpful hints.

**Things you need to know** contains information on getting to Madrid and on travel and daily life in the city.

**Thematic pages** pick out a selection of establishments linked by a common element. These are also shown on a simplified map.

Detailed **maps** are given in the eighth section of the guide: a map of the subway and nine street maps.

## Key

☎ telephone
➡ fax
● price or price range
🕐 opening hours
▣ credit cards accepted
▤ credit cards not accepted
🆅 toll-free number
@ e-mail address

## Access

Ⓜ subway stations
Ⓟ parking
🅿 private parking
♿ facilities for the disabled
🚷 no facilities for the disabled
🚆 train
🚗 car
🚤 boat
🚌 bus

## Hotels

📞 telephone in room
📠 fax in room on request
🍷 minibar
📺 television in room
❄ air-conditioned rooms
🕙 24-hour room service
💂 caretaker
👶 babysitting
➕ meeting room(s)
🐾 no pets
🍽 breakfast
☕ open for tea/coffee
🍴 restaurant
🎵 live music
◉ club
✿ garden, patio or terrace
💪 gym, fitness club
🏊 swimming pool, sauna

## Restaurants

🥗 vegetarian food
🌄 view
👔 smart dress required
🚬 smoking area
🍸 bar

## Museums and galleries

🏛 on-site store(s)
🎫 guided tours
☕ café

## Stores

🏬 branches, outlets

# Getting there

## Pets
To bring a dog or cat into Spain, you need a rabies vaccination certificate and certification, issued within the previous three months, to show that the animal is in good health.

## Electric current
In line with the rest of Europe (except the United Kingdom) the voltage is 220, using two-pin plugs.

## Average temperatures

Summer temperatures range from 12°C to 39°C (53°F to 102°F); winter temperatures are between -8°C and 17°C (18°F and 63°F).

# 46 Things
## you need to Know

### Passports

EU nationals can stay in Spain for up to six months if they have a national identity card, and for an indefinite period if they have a valid passport. US and Canadian tourists visiting Spain for up to three months do not currently require a visa. Others should enquire about visa requirements before departure.

### Health

EU nationals are covered for urgent medical treatment and should take form E111 with them ➡ 15. Non-EU nationals are not covered and are therefore advised to take out adequate medical insurance before departure.

### Driving

Motorists should carry a national or international driving license and a green card issued by their insurers.

## Basic facts

Madrid's only international airport, Madrid-Barajas, lies about 10 miles to the east of the city. Internal flights with Iberia (Spain's national airline) or Aviaco also operate from this airport, forming a network with Spain's major cities, other European capitals (such as London, Paris, Geneva and

# Getting there

## Information

☎ (91) 305 83 43

**Left luggage**
In the arrivals area of the international terminal.

**Tourist office**
☎ (91) 305 86 56
🕐 *Mon.–Fri. 8am–8pm; Sat. 9am–1pm*
In the arrivals area of the international terminal.

**Lost property**
☎ (91) 393 61 19
🕐 *Mon.–Fri. 8am–3pm; Sat. 8am–2pm*
Opposite the left luggage.

**Police**
The office is located near the Iberia desk in the departures area of the international terminal.

## Telephones

Phone boxes take coins and cards on sale at a kiosk next to the Aviaco desk or from automatic dispensers in the international arrivals and domestic departures areas (taking 1000 peseta and 2000 peseta notes).

## Currency exchange

Automatic cash dispensers are located in both domestic and international terminals.

**Argentaria**
☎ (91) 305 55 51
Two offices are open from 6am to 11pm and two open 24 hours (inside the terminals). Exchange rates are slightly higher than in the city.

## Airlines

*American Airlines*
☎ Madrid
*(91) 597 20 68*
☎ UK
*0345 789789*
☎ US
*800-433-7300*
*Aviaco*
*Domestic flights*
☎ *(91) 305 86 85*
*British Airways*
☎ Madrid
*(91) 431 75 75*
☎ UK
*0345 222111*
☎ US
*800-247-9297*
*Iberia*
☎ Madrid
*(91) 240 05 00*
☎ UK
*0345 222111*
☎ US (212) 644 8839

*TWA*
☎ Madrid
*(91) 310 30 94*
☎ UK
*0171-439 0707*
☎ US
*800-892-4141*

## Getting into the city

**Buses**
☎ (91) 431 61 92
Yellow buses run between the airport and Plaza de Colón (the terminus is under the Jardines del Descubrimiento). The journey takes about 30 minutes when traffic flows freely. Buses also stop at Canillejas, Avenida de América, María de Molina and Velázquez.
🕐 *First bus at 4.45am, second at 5.45am, then every 15 minutes from 5.45am to 7am,*

Information 🛈

North terminal

## By plane

Brussels), and with major cities in North America.

then every 10 minutes from 7am until 10pm, and every 30 minutes from 10pm until 1.30am. ● One-way fare: 370 Ptas.

**Taxis**
Outside the airport. Official taxis are white

with a red stripe. A supplement is charged for picking up at the airport and for baggage. All taxis must be equipped with a meter. Fares are

usually shown on a list on one of the rear windows. The fare to Plaza de Colón is about 2000 Ptas, including baggage supplement.

### Airport hotels

**Barajas**
Avenida Logroño 305, 28042
☎ (91) 747 77 00
📠 (91) 747 87 17
24-hour transport.
**Sofitel**
Campo de las Naciones, 28042
☎ (91) 721 00 70
📠 (91) 721 05 15
Courtesy bus.

### Car rental

**Hertz**
☎ (91) 393 72 86
**Avis**
☎ (91) 393 72 22
**Eurodollar Atesa**
☎ (91) 393 72 32
**Europcar**
☎ (91) 393 72 89

## 2nd level

## 1st level
### Check-in

**first floor**
Arrivals

International terminal

P 1

P 6

Domestic terminal

P 2

P 5

Madrid / Barajas Airport **Madrid**

 Parking

 Bus

 Taxis

 Car hire

## Basic facts

RENFE, Spain's national rail company, runs standard and high-speed trains. There are two overnight services from Paris to Madrid. Arriving by car can be straightforward, but roads in the city are congested and parking can be difficult.

# ▶Getting there

## Trains

Information for all train services and all stations can be obtained from a centralized telephone bureau, open 24 hours:

**RENFE**
(*Red Nacional de Ferrocarriles Españolas*)
☎ (91) 328 90 20
Ask about special deals on fares.

**AVE**
Alta Velocidad Española (Spain's own high-speed train).

**Estación de Chamartín**
*Agustín de Foxá, 28036*

Ⓜ *Chamartín*
*Trains for Europe, Spain and Madrid suburbs*
Situated in the north of the city, Chamartín links Madrid with most of Spain and with other countries throughout Europe. The *Cercanías*, or local network, can be the quickest way to travel within the city, and links up with the subway system. An underground train connects Chamartín and Atocha Stations, with stops at Nuevos

Ministerios and Recoletos-Colón. To reach the rest of the city take the subway (the station for this is in the main-line station), taxi or bus (found outside the main-line station).

**Estación de Atocha**
*Plaza Emperador Carlos V, 28012*
Ⓜ *Atocha*
*Trains for Portugal, southern Spain and Madrid suburbs*
Opened in 1851, Atocha is Madrid's oldest station but is also now its most modern. It

consists of two stations: Atocha-Mediodía (for conventional trains) and Puerta de Atocha (departure point for the high-speed AVE). Both connect with the subway. Atocha boasts one of the world's most beautiful waiting rooms ➡ 98. Buses and taxis depart from Plaza Carlos V.

**Norte**
(or Principe Pío)
*Paseo de la Florida, 28008*
Ⓜ *Principe Pío*
Suburban services.

## Cars

Madrid is located at the hub of six main roads radiating across Spain. Distances from the capital are measured from the center of Puerta del Sol. Two ring roads – the M30 and M40 – encircle the city and are less congested than the main thoroughfares of central Madrid. The N1 (Hendaya) enters the city from the north via Plaza de Castilla. The N11 (Figueras) comes from the northeast and joins the Barajas freeway and Avenida de América.

## Traffic information

900 123 505
☎ (91) 742 12 13
🕐 24-hour service

## Gasoline

A liter of premium costs around 120 Ptas. Most gas stations sell premium (*super*) unleaded (*sin plomo*) and diesel (*gasoleo*).

## Safety

Deposit your luggage in the hotel at once on arrival; don't leave it in the car

## Long-distance buses

Cheap but not very fast.

### Estacion Sur de Autobuses

*Méndez Álvaro, corner of Calle Retamar, 28043*
🅼 Méndez Álvaro
☎ (91) 468 42 00
This is the bus station for arrivals and departures of Euroline (international) company buses and Spanish domestic services. For detailed information, the monthly *Guia de Horarios*, which is available from most newsstands, lists all bus routes and times (it has information about train and airline times as well). Tickets for long journeys should be bought in advance from the bus station. Bus services are much reduced on Sundays. When planning a trip, watch out on timetables for the words *diario* (daily) and *domingos y festivos* (Sundays and holidays). The word *laborables* means "workdays and Saturday".

# Getting around

## Subway

☎ *(91) 552 59 09*
The Madrid subway is Europe's third-oldest subway system after London and Paris. *El Metropolitano* was opened in 1919 by King Alfonso XIII. It has 115 stations, carries a million passengers every day and is the quickest way to get around town. It has one major fault: no air-conditioning (installation of this is still at the planning stage).

### Tickets
One-way ticket 135 Ptas for any journey. The pink and white *bonometro diez viajes* entitles you to ten trips for 645 Ptas. Subway tickets can be bought at subway stations, *estancos* (tobacconists), EMT (*Empresa Municipal de Transportes*) information offices, and newsstands. These tickets cannot be used on the buses.

### Timetables
The subway runs daily from 6am to 1.30am.
Rush hours: 7–9.30am; 1.30–2.30pm; 8–9pm.

### Taking the subway
There are ten subway lines, each with its own number and color code. The *circular* line (no. 6, grey) runs around the city, while the rest run from north to south, or from east to west. Pick up a free color map (*plano del metro*) of the subway system from any station.

They are easy to read even if you have no Spanish.

## Buses
The heavy city-center traffic is slow going, but the bus is still a practical way of getting along the main thorough-fares, such as the Paseo de la Castellana. Buses are air-conditioned in summer.

### Tickets
Fares are the same as the subway. However, the ten-trip ticket (*bonobus*) is a long cardboard strip which is punched every time you take the bus. These tickets cannot be bought on the bus. They are available from special sales points; *estancos* (tobacconists), EMT information offices and news-

stands. One-way tickets can be bought on the bus.

### Timetables
Buses run from 6am to midnight. Between midnight and 2am night buses run every 30 minutes from the Puerta del Sol. Between 2am and 5am they run hourly.

### Waiting for the bus
Bus-stops can be recognized by a blue sign showing the number of the bus route, with the main stops listed underneath. Spaniards wait in line for the bus.

### Biobus
A unique Madrid experience – some EMT buses run on vegetable-based fuel (a mixture of diesel and sunflower oil). There are

bus terminus

bus route

plans to extend the same fuel to private cars.

## Taxis

**Radioteléfono**
☎ (91) 547 82 00
**Radio-taxi**
☎ (91) 447 51 80;
(91) 447 32 32
**Tele-taxi**
☎ (91) 445 90 08

**Taking a cab**
Taxis are usually white, but some are black with a red or green diagonal stripe on the side. They can be found at stands near hotels or major tourist attractions, or they can be hailed in the street. A green sign on the windshield shows that a cab is free. A red notice shows which way the driver is heading if they are about to go off duty. The driver will only accept passengers bound for the

same destination. At night, when the subway is closed and there are only night buses, taxis become thin on the ground.

**Fares**
Supplements are charged at night, on Sundays and public holidays, and for picking up at stations, the airport, stadiums and bullrings. Tips (normally about ten per cent) are appreciated but they are not expected. All fees should be clearly posted in the taxi. If, when you reach your destination, you feel you have been overcharged, ask for an official receipt (a white form bearing the city coat-of-arms and perforated with a license number) and send

to city hall: *Área de Circulación y Transportes, Plaza de la Villa 4 28005.*

## Cars

### Parking
Few hotels have private parking lots. Take advantage of those that do by leaving the car there except for excursions out of the city, and getting around by taxi or public transportation. The symbol **P** identifies Madrid's numerous municipal parking lots (Plaza de Colón, Plaza de España y Princesa, Plaza Mayor, Plaza de Santo Domingo, Plaza de las Cortes, Plaza de Santa Ana, Sevilla, Auditorio Nacional and Orense). Madrid is regulated by ORA (*Operación de Regulación del*

*Aparcamiento*), which limit parking to Mon.– Fri. 9am–8pm; Sat. 9am–2pm. Parking permits can be obtained from *estancos*. To save parking fees when renting a car for a day trip or a longer tour, arrange for it delivered to the hotel on the day of departure.

### Car rental
**Atesa**
☎ (91) 559 78 26
**Avis**
☎ (91) 348 03 48
**Europcar**
☎ (91) 555 99 31
**Hertz**
☎ (91) 101 001
**Rentalauto**
☎ (91) 441 36 02

### Breakdown services
**Grúas ADA**
☎ (91) 519 33 00
**Radio-Grúa**
☎ (91) 508 42 42
**Real Automovil Club (RACE)**
☎ (91) 593 33 33

Madrid has plenty of automatic cash machines and places to change money, but many Madrid banks are not open in the afternoons. Stores are generally open until late, but many close for an hour or more at lunchtime. A 24-hour news-stand is located in the Puerta del Sol (2)

# Getting by

## Money

### Currency exchange
235 Ptas = £1,
135 Ptas = $1
(October 1997)
Most banks exchange cash, traveler's checks and Eurocheques.
🕐 Mon.–Fri. 8am–2pm; some banks are open until 4.45pm; some branches are open on Saturday 9am–noon.
Currency can be exchanged in travel agencies, hotels, department stores and 24 hours a day at the airports ➡ 8.

### Tipping
Tip at your discretion in bars and taxis. 50 Ptas to 100 Ptas in modest restaurants, and 5 to 10 % of the bill in upmarket ones. 25 Ptas for restroom attendants and cinema attendants. 100 Ptas per person for ushers in theaters and concert halls.

## Media

### Spanish press
Dailies:
El Mundo; ABC
La Vanguardia;
El País.
Weekly supplements:
Blanco y Negro;
La Revista;
El País Semanal.

### Radio
RNE (state radio, 5 stations)
SER (commercial station, part of the El País and Canal + group)
COPE (station operated by the Catholic Church)
Onda 0 (belongs to a group of charities)

### Television
Public broadcasting channels:
TVE1 and La 2.
Commercial channels:
Canal + (subscription), Antena 3 Televisión and TV 5.
Local channel:
TELE Madrid

## Telephone

### Area codes
91 for calling Madrid from other parts of Spain. Omit area code if calling from inside Madrid.

### Public telephones
Phone boxes take coins or phonecards. Phonecards are available on sale at tobacconists (estancos), news-stands, post offices and 7 Eleven stores.

### Telefónica (3)
Gran Via 30,
28012
🕐 9am–midnight

### International phonecards
Calls from hotels are often higher than standard rates.
Worldtalk
📺 900 97 44 08
● 2000 Ptas
In currency exchange offices Chequepoint (Puerta del Sol). Mainly international calls.

## Mail

Letters can be mailed from large hotels. Post offices are identified by the word correos above the door. Mail boxes have the same word and are yellow. Postage stamps (sellos) can also be bought at tobacco stores.

### Main post office (4)
Palacio de Comunicaciones,
Plaza de Cibeles,
28014
☎ (91) 537 64 94
🕐 Mon.–Fri. 8am–10pm; Sat. 8.30am–2pm (some departments close earlier).

### Neighborhood post offices
Mon.–Fri. 8.30am–8.30pm, some open 8.30am–2.30pm

### Postal rates
To mail a letter weighing 20 g:
21 Ptas (Madrid);
32 Ptas (Spain);
65 Ptas (Europe);
114 Ptas (USA).

(international newspapers are on sale in the city center).

## Getting around

Streets are numbered from the Puerta del Sol end. To ask the way, give the name of the neighborhood (Chamartín, Chamberí, Salamanca or Centro) or the name of the subway station.

## Business hours

### Stores
🕐 9.30am–2pm, 4.30–8pm
Opening times vary in summer.

### Department stores
🕐 Mon.–Sat. 10am–9pm (1st Sunday in the month noon–8pm)

### Museums and churches
Opening hours are very similar to those of stores. But many museums open mornings only on Sundays and close on Mondays.

## Tourist offices

**Oficina Municipal de Turismo**
Plaza Mayor 3, 28012
☎ (91) 588 16 36
🕐 Mon.–Fri. 10am–8pm; Sat. 10am–2pm
This tourist office is secreted under the arcades of the Plaza Mayor (1).

**Oficina de Información Turística de la Comunidad de Madrid**
Duque de Medinaceli 2, 28014
☎ (91) 429 49 51; (91) 429 31 77
🕐 Mon.–Sat. 9am–7pm; Sat.. 9am–1pm

**Patronato Municipal de Turismo**
Mayor 69, 28013
☎ (91) 588 29 00
🕐 Mon.–Thur. 8am–3pm, 4–6pm; Fri. 9am–3pm
**Información Turística General de**

España
☎ (91) 300 600
🕐 Mon.–Fri. 9.30am–5.30pm; Sat.–Sun. 9am–6pm

## Gays and lesbians

**Colectivo de Gais y Lesbianas de Madrid**
Fuencarral 37 primera planta, 28004
☎ (91) 522 45 17
🕐 Mon.–Sat. 6–10pm

**GAI-INFORM**
☎ (91) 523 00 70
🕐 Mon.–Fri. 5–9pm

## Medical care

**Municipal ambulances**
☎ (91) 588 44 00
**Red Cross Ambulances**
☎ (91) 479 93 61

## Pharmacies
🕐 Mon.–Fri. 8am–1.45pm; Sat. 9am–1.45pm
For a list of pharmacies, see Guía del Ocio (the weekly listings

magazine), daily newspapers or pharmacy windows. Some pharmacies stay open late at night, on rotation, each one acting as the farmacia de guardia in turn. To find out which pharmacy is on duty ☎ 098 or look for a notice on the door or window of a pharmacy that is closed. Information about late-night pharmacies can also be found in local newspapers.

## Useful phone numbers

**Fire service (Cuerpo de bomberos)**
☎ 080
**Police (Policia)**
☎ 092
**Ambulance (Ambulancia)**
☎ (91) 588 44 00 or (91) 479 93 61
**Lost property**
☎ (91) 588 43 46

# Where to stay

## Breakfast

Thick, hot chocolate or coffee and pastries filled with cream or jam is usually served. Some hotels also offer Spain's famous *churros*, long fritters made from doughnut batter ➡ 66. Order *café solo* for black coffee, *café cortado* for coffee with a dash of milk, and *café con leche* for a large cup of coffee with plenty of milk.

## Reservations

Reserve rooms in advance. This is advised especially during the high season (*temporada alta*), from June to September and the week before Easter (*Semana Santa*).

**Prices** For all the hotels we list the number of rooms, the price range, the number of suites, the lowest price for a room, and the cost of the cheapest breakfast. Prices given are for a double room inclusive of taxes (VAT at 7%). Most of the large Spanish hotel chains (NH, Meliá or Tryp) and many independent hotels offer special low season and weekend rates.

# Hotels

THE INSIDER'S FAVORITES

## Hotel classification

Madrid offers a wide range of places to stay. *Hotels* listed here carry between one and five stars. *Hostales* are more modest hotels, also graded by a star system. *Pensiones* are family-run guest houses offering the cheapest accommodation.

## Youth hostels

Madrid has two youth hostels. Information and reservations can be obtained from the REAJ (Spanish Youth Hostels Association):
*Red Española de Albergues Juveniles*
*Alcalá 32, 28014*
☎ *(91) 580 42 16*
➡ *(91) 580 42 15*

## In the area

A number of Madrid's great classic hotels lie close to the city's three major museums – Museo del Prado ➡ 96, Museo Thyssen-Bornemisza ➡ 96, and Centro Cultural Reina Sofia ➡ 98. ■ Where to eat ➡ 40 ■ After dark ➡ 70 ➡ 74 ➡ 76 ➡ 78 ■ What to see ➡ 94 ➡ 96

# ► Where to stay

## Ritz (1)
### Plaza de la Lealtad 5, 28014 ☎ (91) 521 28 57 ➡ (91) 532 87 76

Ⓜ *Banco de España* 🅿 *129 rooms* ●●●●● *29 suites 102,000 Ptas* ☯ *2 900 Ptas* 🔲 ⊙ 🔳 📠 📶 🛗 Ⅲ 🍴 *Goya* ➡ *40* 🍸 🖥 🎯 🏋 🏊 ➕ ✂ ✳

This white palace, built under the supervision of King Alfonso XIII and César Ritz and designed by Charles Mewes in 1910, created a revolution in the hotel business. Its elegance, grand public rooms and personal service make it Spain's most celebrated hotel. In summer, the terrace and garden are a popular meeting place for Madrid's smart set.

## Palace (2)
### Plaza de las Cortes 7, 28014 ☎ (91) 360 80 00 ➡ (91) 360 81 00

Ⓜ *Banco de España* 🗣 *396 rooms* ●●●●● *44 suites 128,400 Ptas* ☯ *3200 Ptas* 🔲 🔳 📠 🛗 Ⅲ 🍴 *La Cupola* 🍸 🖥 🎯 🏸 ✳

The Palace, built in 1912, has a much more modern ambience and attitude than its traditional rival, the Ritz. An ambitious renovation program is currently in progress, aimed at restoring the hotel to its former glory and equipping it with state-of-the-art facilities. It has a good Italian restaurant.

## Villa Real (3)
### Plaza de las Cortes 10, 28014 ☎ (91) 420 37 67 ➡ (91) 420 25 47

Ⓜ *Banco de España, Sevilla* 🗣 *115 rooms* ●●●● *12 suites 69,550 Ptas* ☯ *1800 Ptas* 🔲 ⊙ 🔳 📠 🛗 Ⅲ 🍴 🍸 🖥 🏋 🏊 ➕ 🏸

The Villa Real was only recently converted into a hotel. It blends well into this *belle-époque* corner of Madrid, harmonizing with its neighbours, the Spanish Parliament, the Palace and the Ritz. Fine antique furniture and marble bathrooms give it a period feel, but it also has the best in modern fixtures and fittings.

## Gran Hotel Reina Victoria (4)
### Plaza Santa Ana 12, 28014 ☎ (91) 531 45 00 ➡ (91) 522 03 07

Ⓜ *Sol* 🅿 🗣 *201 rooms* ●●●● *4 suites 36,950 Ptas* ☯ *1500 Ptas* 🔲 🔳 📠 🛗 Ⅲ 🍴 🍸 🖥 🎯 🏋 🏊 🏸 ➕ 💈

The Reina Victoria's greatest claim to fame is that it is a favorite haunt of the bullfighting fraternity. Following recent renovations, this early 20th-century building can now boast elegant, modern facilities and interiors.

## Not forgetting

■ **Regina (5)** Alcalá, 19, 28014 ☎ (91) 521 47 25 ➡ (91) 521 47 25 ● ■ **Suecia (6)** Marqués de Casa Riera 4, 28014 ☎ (91) 531 69 00 ➡ (91) 521 71 41 ●●●

■ Where to
shop ➡ 126
➡ 128 ➡ 132

The beautiful cupola
of the Palace,
inaugurated in 1912
by Alfonso XIII,
crowns a *belle-
époque* rotunda.

# Where to stay

## Arosa (7)
### Salud 21, 28013 ☎ (91) 532 16 00 ➡ (91) 531 31 27

Ⓜ Callao, Gran Via 🔆 139 rooms ● Ⓥ 1250 Ptas ▢ ▣ ☎ ⬆ ▥ ▦ Ⓨ ⬜ ✖ ✚

The Arosa is currently undergoing an extensive program of modernization. The hotel shares a building with the largest bookstore in Madrid, Casa del Libro ➡ 132, but the upstairs reception area and separate side entrance help to maintain discretion. There are two restaurants: one, inside the hotel, which is adequate; the other, a few yards away on Calle Jardines, which is more adventurous.

## Gaudí (8)
### Gran Vía 9, 28013 ☎ (91) 531 22 22 ➡ (91) 531 54 69

Ⓜ Gran Via Ⓟ 88 rooms ● 2 suites 26,750 Ptas Ⓥ 1500 Ptas ▢ Ⓞ ▣ ☎ ⬆ ▥ ▦ Ⓨ ⬜ ▨ ✚ ✖ ✚

A small, modern hotel tucked away behind the financial district of Calle Alcalá, the Gaudí is well suited to the business traveler. Unusually for accommodation in this area, the hotel has both a gym and a sauna.

## Style Santo Domingo (9)
### Plaza de Santo Domingo 13, 28013
### ☎ (1) 547 98 00 ➡ (91) 559 22 16

Ⓜ Santo Domingo Ⓟ 120 rooms ● Ⓥ 1350 Ptas ▢ ▣ ☎ ⬆ ▥ ▦ Ⓨ ⬜ ✖ Ⓧ ▨ ✚ @ sdomingo@stnet.es

This small, new hotel situated at the heart of the Gran Vía district is the Madrilenian representative of a new Barcelona-based chain of characterful hotels. Fine furniture, antiques and modern paintings blend well. The lounges retain the impressive granite walls of the apartment block that was once here.

## Tryp Ambassador (10)
### Cuesta de Santo Domingo 5, 28013
### ☎ (91) 541 67 00 ➡ (91) 559 10 40

Ⓜ Ópera, Santo Domingo Ⓟ 182 rooms ●●● 2 suites 61,450 Ptas Ⓥ 1500 Ptas ▢ ▣ ☎ ⬆ ▥ ▦ Ⓨ ⬜ ✖ Ⓧ ▨ ✚

A superb 19th-century mansion in which the Granada de Ega family once lived. It features an interior courtyard, covered by a glass roof, and a conservatory housing a charming restaurant. The Teatro Royal opera house ➡ 92 is located nearby.

## Not forgetting
■ **El Coloso (11)** Leganitos 13, 28013 ☎ (1) 559 76 00 ➡ (91) 547 49 68 ●
■ **Mayorazgo (12)** Flor Baja 3, 28013 ☎ (1) 547 26 00 ➡ (91) 541 24 85 ●

10

7

HOTEL AROSA

7

8

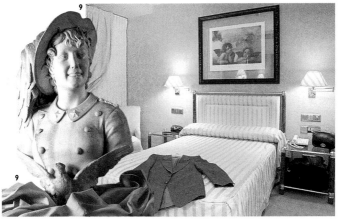

9

9

# ➡ Where to stay

## NH Santo Mauro (13)
### Zurbano 36, 28010 ☎ (91) 319 69 00 ➡ (91) 308 54 77

Ⓜ *Alonso Martínez* 🅿 *26 rooms* ●●●● *11 suites 48,150 Ptas* Ⓥ *2500 Ptas*
▢ ◉ ▣ ☎ 🖪 Ⅲ 🍴 *Belagua* ➡ *52* 🍷 ▢ ✖ 🔧 ≋ 🌊 ★ ➡ *68*

Built as a palace for the dukes of Santo Mauro, this elegant and imposing building was then used by a sequence of foreign embassies before being transformed into a luxury hotel in 1991. The original formal architecture coexists extremely well with the newly designed and fashionably modern interiors. The vast bedrooms that retain their great marble fireplaces have been decorated in a rather unusual style, which is not always to everyone's taste. The glass pavilion serving as entrance to the inner courtyard creates a light and graceful ambience. What was once the library is now a good restaurant, and the gardens and terrace provide an ideal meeting place as well as a delightful setting to rest or relax on a fine day.

## NH Embajada (14)
### Santa Engracia 5, 28010 ☎ (91) 594 02 13 ➡ (91) 447 33 12

Ⓜ *Alonso Martínez* 🅿 *101 rooms* ●● Ⓥ *1700 Ptas* ▢ ▣ ☎ 🖪 Ⅲ 🍴 ▣ 🔧

The ideally-located Embajada has an interesting and attractive design, which dates from the Madrilenian Belle Epoque, when the Spanish regional style with its Castilian and Andalusian features was highly prized. The style achieves its most distinctive expression in the wrought-iron balconies that adorn rooms facing the street. The rooms themselves are modern and functional, in the style of the Spanish chain NH, of which Embajada is a part.

## Tryp Fénix (15)
### Hermosilla 2, 28001 ☎ (91) 431 67 00 ➡ (91) 314 31 56

Ⓜ *Serrano* 🅿 *212 rooms* ●●●● *14 suites 57,250 Ptas* Ⓥ *1550 Ptas* ▢ ▣
☎ 🖪 🍴 🍷 ✖ 🔧 ⊞

The distinctive style of the Tryp Fénix's reception area and its marble-clad lounges evokes the 1950s, a time when the hotel bar was a favorite watering-hole and meeting place of journalists, writers and bankers. Its name derives from the huge bronze imperial phoenix that perches on its rooftop. A few years ago, this venerable if somewhat aging establishment announced a long-awaited relaunch under the wing of the Spanish Tryp chain. The vast bedrooms, which are quiet and well-equipped, have been completely redecorated, and the hotel once again counts itself among the liveliest and most interesting in the capital. Note that the local branch of the Hard Rock Café, which occupies part of the ground floor of the building, has no direct access to the reception area, thereby preserving peace in the hotel.

## Not forgetting
■ **NH Sanvy (16)** Goya 3, 28001 ☎ (01) 576 08 00 ➡ (91) 578 16 39 ●●●

15

14

13

13

16

## In the area

The streets of this eastern section of Madrid are laid out on a grid plan, designed by the Marqués de Salamanca. The area that takes his name is today Madrid's most upmarket residential and shopping area. ■ Where to eat ➡ 44 ➡ 46 ➡ 48 ➡ 50 ■ After dark ➡ 70 ➡ 74 ➡ 80 ■ What to see ➡ 98

# Where to stay

## Villa Magna (17)
### Paseo de la Castellana 22, 28046
### ☎ (91) 576 75 00 ➡ (91) 431 22 86

M Colón 🏨 182 rooms ●●●●● 16 suites 88,810 Ptas 🍽 2950 Ptas ▢ ◐ ▢ 🔧 🛗 Ⅲ 🍴 Tse-Yang, Berceo ➡ 50 Ⓨ 🖥 ✂ ✗ 🎴 ✿ @ villamagna@compuserve.com

The Villa Magna is a modern hotel set in a park of ancient cedars that once belonged to an old palace on the Castellana. The rooms are exceptionally comfortable, and the lounges have a classical English elegance, while the entrance and reception areas reflect a sense of calm opulence that relaxes the senses at the same time as it inspires confidence in the management. This is justified, and the Hyatt chain, which owns the Villa Magna, has excelled itself here in many respects, especially in the culinary field. It has placed Jacques Le Divellec in charge of the exceptional Berceo restaurant, and has also opened a branch of the Geneva-based Chinese restaurant, the Tse-Yang, in the hotel.

## Wellington (18)
### Velázquez 8, 28001 ☎ (91) 575 44 00 ➡ (91) 576 41 64

M Velázquez, Principe de Vergara, Retiro Ⓟ 🏨 296 rooms ●●●● 7 suites 67,300 Ptas 🍽 2200 Ptas ▢ ◐ ▢ ☎ 🔧 Ⅲ 🍴 El Fogón ➡ 46 Ⓨ 🖥 ✂ ✗ 🏊 ✿ 🎴 ✦

This traditional hotel, in the heart of the elegant Salamanca district, has recently been modernized while retaining many of the most-loved features of its former style. Located close to the Ventas bullring ➡ 100, it has long been popular with bullfighters and their followers, and is always full during the Feria de San Isidro in May and June. The service is impeccable, the bedrooms are spacious, and – unusually for Madrid – there is also a swimming pool.

## Gran Hotel Velázquez (19)
### Velázquez 62, 28001 ☎ (91) 575 28 00 ➡ (91) 575 28 09

M Velázquez Ⓟ 🏨 146 rooms ●●● 75 suites 27,500 Ptas 🍽 1475 Ptas ▢ ▢ ☎ 🔧 🍴 Ⓨ 🖥 ✂ 🏊 ✿ 🎴 ✦

The Gran Hotel Velázquez, situated in the heart of the Salamanca district, attracts large numbers of visitors during the major art exhibitions held at the nearby Juan March foundation ➡ 74. It also hosts numerous social activities for a predominantly Spanish clientele. The huge rooms are attractively old-fashioned (1940s in style); the restaurant is adequate if not exceptional. An additional attraction is that tea is served daily in the *salón*.

## Not forgetting

■ **Pintor (20)** Goya 79, 28001 ☎ (91) 435 75 45 ➡ (91) 576 81 57 ●
■ **Convención (21)** O'Donnell 53, 28009 ☎ (91) 574 84 00 ➡ (91) 409 71 60 ●●●

■ Where to
shop ➤ 130 ➤
138 ➤ 140
➤ 144

## In the area

The place for shopaholics and museum-goers, the Castellana is also an architectural showcase. Bullfighting enthusiasts can spend an afternoon at Las Ventas. ■ Where to eat ➡ 50 ■ After dark ➡ 68 ➡ 70 ➡ 72 ➡ 74 ➡ 80 ■ What to see ➡ 100 ➡ 106 ■ Where to shop ➡ 130

# Where to stay

### Emperatriz (22)
**López de Hoyos 4, 28006 ☎ (91) 563 80 88 ➡ (91) 563 98 04**

Ⓜ *Rubén Darío* Ⓟ *153 rooms* ●●●● *3 suites from 48,150 Ptas* Ⓥ *1400 Ptas*
▢◑▢▢▢▢▢▢▢▢▢▢▢▢

Like its neighbor, the Inter-Continental ➡ 28, this comfortable, white-fronted hotel was built in the mid-1950s. It was refurbished in 1996, and the rooms today are bright and cheerful, with pale furniture, soft-colored drapes and three original vestibule panels by Eduardo Vicente, Madrid's chief style interpreter (also responsible for the frescos in the restaurant El Schotis ➡ 36).

### Serrano (23)
**Marqués de Villamejor 8, 28006 ☎ (91) 435 52 00 ➡ (91) 435 48 49**

Ⓜ *Rubén Darío* Ⓟ *30 rooms* ● *4 suites 21,935 Ptas* ▢▢▢▢▢▢▢▢
▢▢

The Serrano is one of Madrid's smallest hotels, valued greatly by its Spanish and Anglo-Saxon regulars for its courteous reception and impeccable service. Though today run by the Husa chain, the hotel has retained its chic, club-like atmosphere. Immaculate bedrooms with newly decorated bathrooms.

### Rafael Ventas (24)
**Alcalá 269, 28027 ☎ (91) 326 16 20 ➡ (91) 926 18 19**

Ⓜ *Carmen* ▢ *110 rooms* ● *1 suite 25,653 Ptas* Ⓥ *975 Ptas* ▢▢▢▢▢
▢▢▢▢▢▢ @ *hotel@rafaelventas.com*

The *fin-de-siècle* version of the Wellington ➡ 24. The new Rafael is closer to the bullring ➡ 100, and numerous toreros and their impresarios have taken to staying in this steel-and-concrete establishment, as have their fans. The rooms are bright and pleasant.

### NH Parque de las Avenidas (25)
**Biarritz 2, 28028 ☎ (91) 361 02 88 ➡ (91) 361 21 62**

Ⓜ *Ventas, Parque de Avenidas* Ⓟ ▢ *198 rooms* ●● *1 suite 19,260 Ptas*
Ⓥ *1500 Ptas* ▢◑▢▢▢▢▢▢▢▢▢▢▢▢

This is one of the most recent of the 12 hotels owned by the NH chain in Madrid, and one of the most successful in terms of its ultra-functional style. The rooms are spacious and comfortable, the small bar is lively, and the modern restaurant serves modern Basque cuisine. Well positioned midway between the bullring ➡ 100 and the residential district of Parque de las Avenidas.

### Not forgetting

■ **Meliáconfort Los Galgos (26)** Claudio Coello 139, 28006 ☎ (91) 562 66 00 ➡ (91) 561 76 62 ●●●
■ **NH Príncipe de Vergara (27)** Príncipe de Vergara 92, 28006 ☎ (91) 563 26 95 ➡ (91) 563 72 53 ●●
■ **Abeba (28)** Alcántara 63, 28006 ☎ (91) 401 16 50 ➡ (91) 402 75 91 ●

27

25

24

24

22

## In the area

This residential district parallels Salamanca, though it has no shopping avenue to compare with that of Calle Serrano. The site of embassies and ministries, it is also home to the charming Museo Sorolla. ■ Where to eat ➡ 52 ➡ 56 ■ After dark ➡ 68 ■ What to see ➡ 106

# Where to stay

### Castellana Inter-Continental (29)
**Paseo de la Castellana 49, 28046**
**☎ (91) 310 02 00 ➡ (91) 308 60 35**

Ⓜ *Rubén Darío* Ⓟ 🅿 *280 rooms* ●●●●● *20 suites 81,855 Ptas* 💹
*2500 Ptas* ▭ ⓪ ◙ 🖥 🔧 ⫼ 🍴 ❗ ✖ ✚ ⊞ ✪ @ *albor@line/pro.es*

The Castellana Inter-Continental has recently been modernized, but it still boasts some of the rarest examples of tasteful 1950s style to be found in Madrid: the red and black marble facings are unique, and the courtyard garden features sculptures by Angel Ferrant – a member of 1950s avant-garde. The garden offers excellent, shaded dining – try the famous club sandwiches. An establishment with a big personality, much loved in Spain.

### Miguel Ángel (30)
**Miguel Ángel 20, 28010 ☎ (91) 442 81 99 ➡ (91) 399 45 19**

Ⓜ *Rubén Darío* Ⓟ 🅿 *263 rooms* ●●●● *30 suites 45,368 Ptas* 💹
*2000 Ptas* ▭ ⓪ ◙ 🖥 🔧 ⫼ 🍴 ❗ ✖ 🥤 ✚ 〰 ✖ ◉ ✪

The Miguel Ángel has a modern exterior combined with an elegant, classical interior that is impressively decorated with Baroque-style carpets and furniture. The well-proportioned bedrooms have recently been refurbished, the service is of a high standard and the management is professional – making this palace on the Castellana one of the most reliable addresses in Madrid. It also boasts a superb indoor swimming pool and gymnasium.

### NH Zurbano (31)
**Zurbano 79-81, 28003 ☎ (91) 441 55 00 ➡ (91) 442 91 48**

Ⓜ *Rubén Darío* 🅿 *264 rooms* ●● *10 suites 31,030 Ptas* 💹 *1700 Ptas* ▭ ◙
🖥 🔧 ⫼ 🍴 ❗ ✖ ✚

Vuelta de España drivers and other professional sporting teams often stay in this comfortable, NH-style hotel close to the Castellana. Its sporting reputation means that it is livelier and more colorful than many of the other hotels in the chain.

### Style Esculltor (32)
**Miguel Ángel 3, 28010 ☎ (91) 310 42 03 ➡ (91) 319 25 84**

Ⓜ *Ruben Darío* 🅿 *47 rooms* ●●●● *2 suites 37,450 Ptas* 💹 *1300 Ptas* ▭ ◙
🖥 🔧 ⫼ 🍴 ❗ ✖ 〰 ✚

A small, basic but comfortable hotel, the Style Esculltor looks out over the Glorieta Rubén Darío, now the most expensive residential square in town.

## Not forgetting

■ **NH Prisma (33)** Santa Engracia 120, 28003 ☎ (91) 441 93 77
➡ (91) 442 58 51 ●

29

30

Statue of Gregorio Marañón, endocrinologist and Madrid historian.

30

30

29

32

## In the area

The wide thoroughfare of the Paseo de la Castellana is lined with government ministries and hotels geared toward the business traveler. Two skyscrapers – the 43-story Torre Picasso and the twin-towered Puerta de Europa – stand as symbols of Madrid's modernity.

# ➡ Where to stay

### Meliá Castilla (34)
**Capitán Haya 43, 28020** ☎ **(91) 567 50 00** ➠ **(91) 567 52 51**

Ⓜ *Plaza de Castilla* 🅿 🔆 *896 rooms* ●●●●● *14 46,350 Ptas* 🎿 *2300 Ptas*
🔲 🔘 🔲 🔲 🔲 🔲 🔲 🔲 🔲 🔲 🔲 🔲 🔲 🔲 ➠ *82*

An uninspiring skyscraper from the outside, the Meliá Castilla rewards closer inspection. It offers attentive service, comfortable, tastefully decorated rooms, two reputable restaurants and a famous cabaret venue and nightclub.

### Aitana (35)
**Paseo de de la Castellana 152, 28046**
☎ **(91) 344 11 42** ➠ **(91) 457 07 81**

Ⓜ *Lima, Cuzco* 🔆 *109 rooms* ● *2 suites from 19,046 Ptas* 🎿 *750 Ptas* 🔲 🔲
🔲 🔲 🔲 🔲 🔲 🔲 🔲 🔲

This unassuming hotel opposite the Ministry of Defence is only a stone's throw from the Azca complex and the Palacio de Congresos ➠ 108. The Aitana has a loyal clientele of regular business travelers and offers good personal service. The 1970s-style rooms, spread over ten stories, are beginning to date, but are still welcoming. Those overlooking Calle Profesor Waksmann are quieter than those on the Castellana.

### Holiday Inn (36)
**Plaza de Carlos Trías Beltrán 4, 28020**
☎ **(91) 456 80 00** ➠ **(91) 456 80 01**

Ⓜ *Nuevos Ministerios, Lima* 🅿 🔆 *282 rooms* ● *31 suites 27,750 Ptas* 🎿
*2,065 Ptas* 🔲 🔲 🔲 🔲 🔲 🔲 🔲 🔲 🔲 🔲 🔲 🔲

A modern building, ideally located close to the Torre Picasso, Spain's highest skyscraper, opposite the Real Madrid stadium and the Palacio de Congresos, and right in the heart of Azca, Madrid's largest business complex ➠ 108. American-style comfort: large beds, a swimming pool, rooftop solarium and a gym.

### Castilla Plaza (37)
**Paseo de la Castellana 220, 28046**
☎ **(91) 323 11 86** ➠ **(91) 315 54 06**

Ⓜ *Plaza de Castilla* 🔆 *186 rooms* ●●● *6 suites 23,700 Ptas* 🎿 *1150 Ptas* 🔲
🔲 🔲 🔲 🔲 🔲 🔲 🔲 🔲 🔲 🔲

This recently opened hotel (1994) lies at the foot of the two leaning towers of the Puerta de Europa ➠ 108, modern Madrid's most talked-about landmark. It is well equipped, and the ultra-modern rooms are softened by wooden fittings and plants. A tapas bar with a surprisingly good menu adds an unexpected, but welcome, Madrilenian touch.

## Not forgetting

■ **Orense (38)** Orense 38, 28020 ☎ (91) 597 15 68 ➠ (91) 597 12 95 ●●●
■ **Cuzco (39)** Paseo de la Castellana 133, 28046 ☎ (91) 556 06 00
➠ (91) 556 03 72 ●●●

The Real Madrid district is a prime example of the Madrilenian 'boom' of the 1960s, when anarchic urban planning schemes were implemented. Both a shopping district and a residential area, its real treasures, tucked away at its center, are the *colonias*, with their villas and secluded gardens.

# Where to stay

## Eurobuilding (40)
**Padre Damián 23, 28023 ☎ (91) 345 45 00 ➡ (91) 345 45 76**

Ⓜ *Cuzco* 🅿 480 rooms ●●●●● *52 suites 38,300 Ptas* 🅥 *2000 Ptas* ▯

Occupying an entire block of houses just off the Castellana, this is more of a city than a hotel. If this may seem a disadvantage to those looking for a more intimate environment, this can be countered by the advantages of the impressive raised terrace-garden, with a beautiful outdoor pool – a rarity in Madrid – which combine to give Eurobuilding the edge over its competitors. In addition, the hotel has numerous conference rooms, restaurants, shops, the most famous bridge club in Madrid, and a renowned debating society. Many business travelers return here again and again for the hotel's impressive of facilities.

## La Residencia de El Viso (41)
**Nervión 8, 28002 ☎ (91) 564 03 70 ➡ (91) 564 19 65**

Ⓜ *República de Argentina* 🅿 *12 rooms* ● 🅥 *750 Ptas* ▯ @ elviso@estancias.es

La Residencia de El Viso is a remarkable cubist-style, salmon-pink villa that typifies the rationalist architecture of the 1930s. In addition to this architectural distinction, the hotel provides a green and quiet refuge from the noisy, bustling capital, even though it is situated right in the city center. Its small bedrooms are functional and modern. A garden-view restaurant serves fresh market produce.

## Aristos (42)
**Avenida Pío XII 34, 28016 ☎ (91) 345 04 50 ➡ (91) 345 10 23**

Ⓜ *Pío XII* 🅿 *24 rooms* ●● *1 suite 24,650 Ptas* 🅥 *800 Ptas* ▯ *El Chaflán* ▯ *El Chaflán*

Situated at the end of an avenue that once marked the northern limits of the city, the Aristos has a deserved reputation as a charming place to stay for a romantic visit to Madrid. The rooms are impeccable, the garden delightful, and the restaurant excellent. Since the early 1990s, a burgeoning business district on the nearby M30 bypass has attracted a lively new clientele to this small hotel.

## NH Habana (43)
**Paseo de la Habana 73, 28036 ☎ (91) 345 82 84 ➡ (91) 457 75 79**

Ⓜ *Colombia* 🅿 *157 rooms* ●●● 🅥 *1700 Ptas* ▯

Frequented especially by sportsmen and by Basque and Catalan business travelers, the Habana is the Charmartín representative of the ubiquitous NH hotel group. This establishment is modern and is also more luxurious than others in the chain. One attraction for sports enthusiasts is that the concierge has an amazing ability to procure tickets for even the most oversubscribed Real Madrid football matches ➡ 108.

■ Where to eat ➡ 36 ➡ 60 ➡ 64
■ After dark ➡ 70 ➡ 72 ■ What to
see ➡ 108 ■ Where to shop ➡ 142

41

41

42

41

The Bauhaus and art deco
movements have left their
imprint on the El Viso area.

41

**Tipping**
Although service (12% of the total)
is always included in the bill, it is
usual to leave at least 5% more.

# ➡ Where to eat

**IVA**
Some restaurants give prices
inclusive of IVA (VAT at 7%); others
add it to the total. The menu should
state whether or not IVA is included.

**Parking**
It is not unusual for restaurants, especially the
upmarket kind, to have doormen to park diners'
cars for them. Otherwise parking is difficult in
the narrow, winding streets of old Madrid.

## Busy times

It is worth reserving a table, especially at lunchtime. The locals take a very late lunch (often not until around 2.30pm), but they no longer dine around midnight like they used to, preferring to eat around 9.30pm. Nevertheless, restaurants are quite accustomed to taking earlier reservations from foreign visitors.

# 73
# Restaurants

THE INSIDER'S FAVORITES

## Basic facts

In the 19th century, tascas were the wine leftovers used to concoct such basic dishes as the *cocido*, a stew made from cabbage, *chorizo* (spicy sausage) and chickpeas. The word 'tasca' is now applied to small restaurants, called *tascas ilustradas*. There is still a large number of these in Madrid, often

# Where to eat

## Casa Lucio (1)
### Cava Baja 35, 28005 ☎ (91) 365 32 52 ➡ (91) 366 48 66

**M** *La Latina* ●●● ▯ ◔ *Mon.–Fri., Sun. 1.15–3.45pm, 9pm–midnight; Sat. 9–11.30pm; closed in August* **Y**

This historic inn was renovated in the 1970s by the great Lucio Blázquez, who has transformed it into one of the best-known and most fashionable Madrilenian restaurants. The owner is a colorful character of such renown that he has been made the subject of a book, a copy of which he is proud to produce. The established ritual for most regulars begins with a plate of *patatas revolconas* (sautéd potatoes with scrambled eggs), followed by red meat, milk-fed roast lamb or fried hake, washed down by a carafe of Valdepeñas. To soak up the atmosphere, ask for a table in the main brick-vaulted dining room.

## El Schotis (2)
### Cava Baja 11, 28005 ☎ (91) 365 32 30 ➡ (91) 365 72 44

**M** *Tirso de Molina* ●●● ▯ ◔ *Mon.–Sat. 1–4.30pm, 8.30pm–12.30am; Sun. 1–4.30pm* **Y**

The splendid frescos depicting scenes from old Madrid (painted by Eduardo Vicente in the 1940s) add a lively touch to this *tasca*, a local-style restaurant which has influenced numerous other similar eating houses in the area. The waiters are 'old-timers' who have become co-owners and are most attentive. Try the stuffed sweet peppers and excellent red meats.

## La Fuencisla (3)
### San Mateo 4, 28004 ☎ (91) 521 61 86

**M** *Tribunal* ●● ▯ ◔ *Mon.–Sat. 1.30–4pm, 7pm–1am; closed in August* **Y**

Modern paintings of questionable artistic merit and bullfighting mementoes adorn the walls of this tiny dining room. Señor and Señora De Frutos serve up excellent home cooking, which reflects the traditions of Segovia ➡ 120, their native town. While the proprietor presides over the front-of-house, as he has for the last 40 years or so, his wife creates meals in the kitchen. Try the grilled chops of milk-fed lamb or oven-baked *ventresca* (fillet) of tuna. The Rioja wines are exceptional.

## De la Riva (4)
### Cochabamba 13, 28016 ☎ (91) 458 89 54

**M** *Colombia* ●● ▯ ◔ *Mon.–Fri. 1.30–6pm; closed in August*

De la Riva has moved to the north of the city where, in a nondescript building in the modern district of Chamartín, its eponymous owner has re-created the atmosphere of a traditional *tasca*. When ordering, trust his advice as he recites the dishes of the day, among them *chipirones* (squid) in their ink, roasted fillet of veal, and the famous Castilian conger eel. This *tasca* is closed in the evenings.

plainly decorated with colored *azulejos,* (ceramic tiles), offering an atmospheric place to meet but little in the way of comfort.

4

Restaurante

**CASA LUCIO**

Lucio Blázquez makes a point of offering his customers those tables at which famous guests have sat.

2

## In the area

Plaza Mayor, nestling between the Hapsburg district and the old working-class neighborhoods of Madrid, is a splendid architectural ensemble. From the 17th to the 20th centuries, it was the hub of the city, and many old stores remain. ■ Where to stay ➡ 20 ■ After dark

# Where to eat

## Botín (5)
**Cuchilleros 17, 28005 ☎ ( 91) 366 42 17 ➡ (91) 366 84 94**

Ⓜ Sol, Tirso de Molina **Castilian cuisine** ●● ▭ Ⓒ daily 1–4pm, 8pm–midnight

This traditional establishment, founded in 1725, was entered in the *Guiness Book of Records* as 'the oldest restaurant in the world'. Happily, though, its four stories, exposed beams, wood oven and Castilian decoration in no way resemble a dusty museum. Delicious milk-fed lamb and roasted suckling pig are served to a mixed clientele of tourists and Madrileños.

## Caripén (6)
**Plaza de la Marina Española 4, 28013 ☎ (91) 541 11 77**

Ⓜ Santo Domingo **French bistro cuisine** ●● ▭ Ⓒ Mon.–Sat. 9pm–3am

In a genuine art deco dining room Daniel Boute serves up the best French-style bistro cooking in Madrid. The Caripén is also one of the Madrid's most appealing restaurants in another sense, because you can eat here well after midnight when most other restaurants have closed. Sample specialties such as mussels in a cream sauce, excellent and copious fresh pasta, deliciously fresh steak tartare, mouth-watering skate in black butter and, to round out the meal, a superlative Tarte Tatin. The cellar has some good French wines including a wonderful, reasonably priced vintage Médoc.

## La Esquina del Real (7)
**Amnistía 2, 28013 ☎ (91) 559 43 09**

Ⓜ Ópera **French cuisine** ●●● ▭ Ⓒ Mon.–Fri. 2–4pm, 9.30pm–midnight; Sat. 8pm–midnight; closed Aug. 11–24

Located a few yards from the Teatro Real ➡ 92, the Esquina del Real is one of Madrid's well-kept culinary secrets. The 17th-century building is one of the oldest in Madrid, with impressive granite walls that are nearly six feet thick. Marcel Margossian serves classic and resolutely French dishes, including Dublin Bay prawns with raspberry vinegar, delicious home-made foie gras, fricassée of veal sweetbreads, and as a specialty, flambéd Tarte Tatin.

## Not forgetting

■ **Bajamar (8)** Gran Vía 78, 28013 ☎ (91) 548 48 18 ●●●●● *Sublime fish and shellfish, simply cooked. Expensive.*
■ **Entre Suspiro y Suspiro (9)** Plaza de la Marina Española 4, 28013 ☎ (91) 542 06 44 ●● *Genuine Mexican home cooking – a far cry from the local 'Tex Mex'.*
■ **La Bola (10)** Bola 5, 28013 ☎ (91) 547 69 30 ● *A Taberna (inn) with an old-style tasca atmosphere ➡ 36. Serves up an excellent cocido madrileño (Madrilenian stew).*
■ **Cornucopia (11)** Flora 1, 28013 ☎ (91) 547 64 65 ●● *Debora Hansen (from Boston) serves up New England clam chowder and other more modern Spanish dishes in this authentic belle époque interior.*

**Ópera**  E B2

➥ 68 ➥ 80 ■ What to see
➥ 92 ➥ 102 ■ Where to
shop ➥ 126 ➥ 128 ➥ 134 ➥
144

39

# Where to eat

## Viridiana (12)
**Juan de Mena 14, 28014 Madrid** ☎ **(91) 523 44 78** ➡ **(91) 532 42 74**

Ⓜ *Retiro* **Modern Castilian cuisine** ●●● ▭ 🕐 *Mon.–Sat. 1.30–4pm, 9pm–midnight; closed Easter week, August, Christmas*

Everything here is dedicated to the memory of Luis Buñuel. The movie-mad proprietor Abraham García is a colorful character, always on the look out for new and exotic ingredients and techniques (the menu changes fortnightly), while remaining rooted in his native Castile. The result is the most inventive cuisine in Madrid. The cellar is exceptional, stocked with wines from around the world.

## El Cenador del Prado (13)
**Prado 4, 28014** ☎ **(91) 429 15 61** ➡ **(91) 369 04 55**

Ⓜ *Sevilla* **Mediterranean cuisine** ●●● ▭ 🕐 *Mon.–Fri. 1.45–4pm, 9pm–midnight; Sat. 9pm–midnight; closed first week in August*

Abandoning their haute cuisine, the Herranz brothers have opted for a cheaper, neo-Madrilenian version. Yet their clam and potato ragout, venison medallions with quince jelly, and chocolate stuffed with pear ice-cream never disappoint, and the three dining rooms are sumptuous.

## Errota-Zar (14)
**Jovellanos 3, 28014** ☎ **(91) 531 25 64** ➡ **(91) 531 25 64**

Ⓜ *Banco de España, Sevilla* **Basque cuisine** ●●● ▭ 🕐 *Mon.–Sat. 1–4pm, 9pm–midnight; closed Easter week*

Errota-Zar belongs to Euskal Etxea, the home of Basque cuisine in Madrid. In this plush, traditional setting, the Olano family serves up excellent meats and popular Basque dishes, such as Tolosa kidney beans, almond cardoons, and Bay of Biscay cod.

## Paradis Madrid (15)
**Marqués de Cubas 14, 28014** ☎ **(91) 429 73 03** ➡ **(91) 429 32 95**

Ⓜ *Banco de España* **Catalan cuisine** ●●● ▭ 🕐 *Mon.–Fri. 1.30–4pm, 9pm–midnight; Sat. 9pm–midnight; closed Easter week, August, public holidays*

With its Catalan-style décor and old mosaic-tiled floor, this Madrid branch of the Barcelona-based restaurant chain is a worthy ambassador of the cuisine and wines of the principality: broad beans sautéed with squid, sea bream cooked on a hot slate, Catalan cream, Penedés and Priorato wines.

**Not forgetting**
■ **Goya (16)** Hotel Ritz, Plaza de la Lealtad 5, 28014 ☎ (91) 521 28 57 ●●●● *A splendid wood-paneled dining room overlooking Madrid's most beautiful summer garden. Cocido, callos (tripe) a la madrileña…the menu changes daily.*
■ **La Vaca Verónica (17)** Moratín 38, 28014 ☎ (91) 429 78 27 ●● *Decorated in the style of a Madrid mansion of the early 1900s. Featured on the menu are salads, bourgeois dishes and excellent Argentinian meats.*

Where to
shop ➡ 128
➡ 132

```
                    C. de la Reina
        G r a n      12   C. de Alcalá
    22            9 8       Banco de M
C. Caballero de Gracia   V i a  España   Plaza de
   21                       15  Cibeles
      de            6
         M  Sevilla  Casa Riera  Alcalá     C. de Montalbán
   10 5                 19                   Alfonso XI
C. de Sevilla  C. Cedaceros  Calle de los Madrazo  C. Juan de Alarcón  12
Crt. de San                25  14          C. Antonio Maura
   13  Jerónimo   Calle de Zorrilla   Plaza
   23  8    Pl. de las  15  de la
      12  Cortes  14     Lealtad   19
   Pl.  3          17  1 16  Calle Felipe IV
Sta.  2           Plaza Cánovas
Ana  22  Calle del Prado   del Castillo  13  18
   9  Calle de Cervantes         MUSEO
Calle  Calle  de León  Lope de Vega  DEL  C. de Moreto
   de las  Huertas         PRADO
C. Magdalena  20  Calle de Sta. Maria  Pl. Platería  Pl. de  C. Espalter
A. Martín  M Atocha  Calle de Moratín  Martínez  Murillo  23
   C. del Olmo  Calle  C. Verónica  JARDIN
          Gobernador   BOTANICO
```

16                                                    16

14

17

17

12

## In the area

Cibeles is dominated by two symbols of Madrid – the fountain of Cybele, showing the goddess in a chariot, and the granite Puerta de Alcalá. ■ Where to stay ➡ 18 ➡ 20 ■ After dark ➡ 72 ➡ 74 ➡ 76 ■ What to see ➡ 94 ➡ 96 ➡ 98 ■ Where to shop ➡ 132 ➡ 138

 # Where to eat

### San Carlo (18)
**Barquillo 10, 28004 ☎ (91) 522 79 88 ➡ (91) 522 73 01**

M *Banco de España* **Modern Italian cuisine** ●● ☐ ⊙ *daily 1–4.30pm, 9–11.30pm* ⊻

A newcomer in a category that is well represented but often disappointing in Madrid, the San Carlo offers authentic trans-alpine cooking. The impressive interior calls to mind the Teatro San Carlo in Naples, a city that was for a long time ruled by Spain. Light pizzas are served up in the first room; in the second, a modestly updated Italian cuisine, with fresh tomato sauce and beef *tagliata* with rocket. Musical evenings at weekends.

### Nicolás (19)
**Villalar 4, 28001 ☎ (91) 431 77 37 ➡ (91) 431 77 37**

M *Banco de España, Retiro* **Creative Spanish cuisine** ●● ☐ ⊙ *Tues.–Sat. 1.30–4pm, 9pm–midnight; closed Easter week, August*

Formerly a bistro in a working-class neighborhood, Nicolás has become a comfortable restaurant with minimalist decor and Guinovart prints on the walls. The cuisine served up by Juan José Méndez is as simple and elegant as ever: lamb sweetbreads in breadcrumbs, cassoulet of squid and chickpeas, duck's liver with pears, and perfect cod *ajoarriero* (in garlic).

### La Gamella (20)
**Alfonso XII 4, 28004 ☎ (91) 532 45 09 ➡ (91) 523 34 90**

M *Retiro* **Spanish and American cuisine** ●●●● ☐ ⊙ *Mon.–Fri. 1.30–4pm, 9pm–midnight; Sat. 9pm–midnight; closed Easter week, 15 days in August*

A truly postmodern eating house with scarlet walls. The restaurant, run by Richard Stephens, combines the best of Spanish and American cuisine. The latter is fairly predictable (steak tartare with bourbon, excellent cheesecake), while the former is more inventive (eggplant with Manchego cheese and Xérès brandy and a tomato coulis).

### Horcher (21)
**Alfonso XII 6, 28014 ☎ (91) 522 07 31 ➡ (91) 522 34 90**

M *Retiro* **Traditional German cuisine** ●●●● ☐ ⊙ *Mon.–Fri. 1.30–4pm, 8.30pm–midnight; Sat. 8.30pm–midnight; closed in August*

The Horchers arrived in Madrid in 1943, when allied bombs were falling on the family restaurant in Berlin. A cozy conservative Saxon atmosphere in which to sample traditional German cuisine served up by Carlos Horcher: herrings with *kartoffelpuffer*, game, Viennese strudels.

### Not forgetting

■ **Club 31 (22)** Alcalá 58, 28014 ☎ (91) 531 00 92 ●●●●●
*International cuisine with a classic finish served up in a luxury-style canteen to a well-heeled clientele.*

NICOLAS
Villalar, 4
Teléfono 431 77 37
28001 Madrid

## In the area

This square, commemorating the discovery of America, and the nearby shopping street of Génova are presided over by the Torres Heron, twin towers linked by an incongruous green 'hat'. ■ Where to stay ➡ 22 ■ After dark ➡ 68 ➡ 72 ➡ 76 ➡ 78 ➡ 84 ■ What to see ➡ 104

# Where to eat

### Jockey (23)
**Amador de los Ríos 6, 28010 ☎ (91) 319 24 35 ➡ (91) 319 24 35**

Ⓜ *Colón* **Classic Spanish and French cuisine** ●●●●● ☐ 🕐 *Mon.–Fri. 1–4pm, 9pm–midnight; Sat. 9pm–midnight; closed public holidays, August*

The green, velvet benches and equestrian prints have been here since the restaurant opened in 1945. For over half a century, it has maintained its position at the top of Madrid's restaurant league under the direction of the Cortés family. The cuisine is ultra-conservative, but the well-roasted fatted chicken served up by chef Jesús Barbolla has definite appeal. Private dining rooms, and a clientele of bankers and politicians.

### Ciao Madrid (24)
**Argensola 7, 28004 Madrid ☎ (91) 308 25 19 ➡ (91) 429 32 95**

Ⓜ *Alonso Martínez* **Italian trattoria** ●●● ☐ 🕐 *Mon.–Fri. 1.30–3.45pm, 9.30pm–midnight; Sat. 9.30pm–midnight; closed September* Ⓜ *Apodaca 20, 28004 ☎ (91) 447 00 36*

When it comes to authentic, family-run Italian *trattorias*, Ciao Madrid wins hands down. The decor is unremarkable and the service brisk, but the cooking is good and ranges from pasta (*gnocchi al pesto* and ravioli with zucchini) to meat dishes (carpaccio and a robust *cotechino* with lentils). The cellar stocks a good Rosso di Montalcino. The related establishment on Calle Apocada serves excellent pizzas.

### El Mentidero de la Villa (25)
**Santo Tomé 6, 28004 ☎ (91) 308 12 85 ➡ (91) 319 87 92**

Ⓜ *Alonso Martínez* **Modern Franco-Spanish cooking** ●●● ☐ 🕐 *Mon.–Fri. 1.30–4pm, 9pm–midnight; Sat. 9pm–midnight; closed Aug. 15–31*

The charming proprietor Mario Martínez has created a fairy-tale interior with the aid of *trompe l'oeil* murals and carousel horses. The culinary style is modern Franco-Spanish, featuring unusual but simple fish dishes and perfect cuts of lamb. An excellent cellar stocked with Spanish wines.

### Al Mounia (26)
**Recoletos 5, 28001 ☎ (91) 435 08 28**

Ⓜ *Colón, Banco de España* **Moroccan cuisine** ●●● ☐ 🕐 *Tues.–Sat. 1.30–4pm, 9–11.30pm*

The ornate decorative motifs conceived by Moroccan craftsmen are alone worth a visit, but the best North African restaurant in Madrid has other delights to offer: the *b'stella etheree* (Castilian lamb prepared Moroccan-style) is excellent and the couscous is light and flavorsome. The wines are expensive but not of the standard of the food.

## Not forgetting

■ **La Alpargatería (27)** Hermosilla 7, 28001 ☎ (91) 577 43 45 ●
*Italian-style pasta, Argentinian beef and a no-fuss atmosphere. Modest prices.*
■ **Pelotari (28)** Recoletos 3, 28001 ☎ (91) 578 24 97 ●●●
*Classic Basque cuisine with excellent beef grills.*

■ Where to shop ➡
136

26

At Al Mounia the interior, atmosphere and food will transport you to the Maghreb. An essential 'detour' for those wanting to learn more about Spanish history while in Madrid.

26

24

28

## In the area

Located north of Retiro Park, this part of the Salamanca district has developed into an upmarket shopping area specializing in designer items and luxury goods. It is here that the most prestigious commercial art galleries are located.

# Where to eat

## El Amparo (29)
**Puigcerdá 8, 28001 ☎ (91) 431 64 56 ➡ (91) 575 54 91**

Ⓜ *Goya* **Modern Spanish cuisine** ●●●●● ▤ ◯ *Mon.–Sat. 1.30–3.30pm, 9–11.30pm; closed Aug. 11–17*

One of the finest and most innovative restaurants in Madrid, El Amparo was relaunched following the arrival as culinary adviser of Martín Berasategui, one of the most outstanding young chefs to emerge from the Basque Country in recent years. Several intimate dining areas are laid out on different levels around a covered interior courtyard. Choose from the prawn and wild mushroom salad, the white tuna and lobster mousse or the grilled turbot with spinach and a shellfish-and-saffron couli. The menu also includes a slection of choice cuts of meat. Luis Miguel Martín, one of the best sommeliers in Madrid, runs a well-stocked wine cellar that includes bottles of *prioratos* and *riberas*, some of the latest labels to cause a stir.

## La Paloma (30)
**Jorge Juan 39, 28001 ☎ (91) 576 86 92**

Ⓜ *Goya, Vergara* **Creative gourmet cuisine** ●●●● ▤ ◯ *Mon.–Sat. 1.30–4pm, 9–11.45pm; closed Easter week, August, public holidays*

Segundo Alonso was head chef at El Amparo, but has now opened his own restaurant nearby. La Paloma is less luxurious, and not as beautifully decorated, but the menu is less expensive, while the service is impeccable, and Alonso's cooking is as robust and appealing as ever. This undisputed master of variety meats – notably pigs' trotters – excels equally at wood pigeon stuffed with foie gras, lasagna with spider crab and spinach and watercress coulis. He also creates some mouthwatering desserts.

## Teatriz (31)
**Hermosilla 15, 28001 ☎ (91) 577 53 79**

Ⓜ *Serrano* **Italian cuisine** ●●● ▤ ◯ *daily 1.30–4pm, 9pm–1am; closed in August* Ⓨ ◯

A fashionable restaurant where many of the regulars are being squeezed out by crowds of newcomers visiting this old theater – often less for its superb cuisine than for its extraordinary modern decor, designed by Philippe Starck in the early 1990s. Not least among its wonders must be a visit to the *servicios* (W.C.s), in the center of which stands a throne-like fountain of gold, marble and silver, all bathed in a bluish light – you could be forgiven for thinking this was a nightclub.

## Not forgetting

■ **La Trainera (32)** Lagasca 60, 28001 ☎ (91) 576 05 75 ●●●●
*A rustic tasca serving up excellent seafood. A good Jabugo (cured ham) for meat-lovers, plus langoustines, sole and turbot, all delicately prepared.*
■ **El Fogón (33)** Hôtel Wellington, Villanueva 34, 28001 ☎ (91) 575 44 00
●● *A good hotel restaurant serving up classic Spanish dishes. Service is smooth.*

29

33

29

32

31

The Teatriz (above) was designed by Philippe Starck, the French architect and designer, who attaches great symbolic importance to shapes and spaces.

## In the area

Goya is a large upmarket residential district, much of it built in the early 1900s. Its northern perimeter is marked by a splendid plaza dedicated to Salamanca – the man behind this urban grid-plan. The district stretches south to Retiro Park, and is also the most direct route to the bullring.

# Where to eat

### El Buey I (34)
**General Pardiñas 10, 28001 ☎ (91) 431 44 92**

M *Príncipe de Vergara* **Grills** ●● ▣ ◷ *daily 1–4pm, 9pm–midnight*

Despite its origin as a 'formula' restaurant, El Buey I has managed to rise above the negative connotations of such a label, as the clientele attests. The long, narrow dining room, resembling a railroad dining-car, is always packed. Diners flock here for the tender slabs of beef roasted over a wood fire, served up in unusually generous portions. A good *estofado de ternera* (beef stew) helps vary the meat theme, but beef is not the only ingredient on the menu. There is onion soup as a starter, a choice of specials (the game and mushroom lasagna is excellent), and lemon sorbet to finish off with, all washed down with a good Duero *ribera* house wine.

### Gargantuel (35)
**Menorca 35, 28009 ☎ (91) 504 68 88 ➡ (91) 504 69 86**

M *Retiro* **Regional specialties** ●● ▣ ◷ *Mon.–Sat. 1.30–5pm, 9pm–1.30am; Sun. 1.30–4pm*

For more than a decade, Rafael Rincón has been opening bistro-like outlets in different parts of Madrid. Now he has opened more comfortable premises. Gargantuel is a basic and unpretentious restaurant, where Carmen Magro serves up regional dishes from all over Spain. Among these, dishes such as the *atascaburras* from La Mancha are hard to find anywhere, even in their region of origin. This is Gargantuel's strong point, though the restaurant also offers a menu for those who prefer a simple salad or fish dish. The lunchtime menu changes daily, and the interesting wine list is updated regularly.

### Castelló 9 (36)
**Castelló 9, 28001 ☎ (91) 435 91 34 ➡ (91) 435 91 34**

M *Príncipe de Vergara* **Modern Spanish cuisine** ●●●●● ▣ ◷ *Mon.–Sat. 1.30–4pm, 9pm–midnight; closed Easter week, public holidays*

Castelló 9 provides a smart setting in which to sample Franco-Spanish food in the style of the Jockey genre ➡ 44. For particular specialties, try the wild-mushroom omelette with lobster or the hake tartare with caviar; neither will disappoint.

### El Pescador (37)
**José Ortega y Gasset 75, 28006 ☎ (91) 402 12 90 ➡ (91) 401 30 26**

M *Lista* **Fish and shellfish** ●●● ▣ ◷ *Mon.–Sat. 1–4pm, 8.30pm–midnight; closed Easter week, August*

The rustic setting of El Pescador, with fishing nets hanging from the ceiling, conjures up images of the dockside taverns of Spain's northern ports. Here, you can sample the same seafood cooking as at O'Pazo ➡ 56, but at slightly lower prices. Enormous fresh sole served up *lenguado Evaristo*-style is unbeatable.

## In the area

An extension of the shopping district of Serrano, this is the most attractive section of the Castellana. ■ Where to stay ➡ 24 ➡ 26 ➡ 28 ■ After dark ➡ 68 ➡ 70 ➡ 72 ➡ 74 ➡ 80 ■ What to see ➡ 106 ■ Where to shop ➡ 130 ➡ 140

# Where to eat

## Suntory (38)
### Castellana 36-38, 28046 ☎ (91) 577 37 34 ➡ (91) 577 44 55

Ⓜ *Rubén Darío* **Japanese cuisine** ●●●●● ▭ ◯ *Mon.–Sat. 1.30–3.30pm, 8.30–11.30pm; closed public holidays*

With its minimalist décor and maximally attentive service, this exceptional restaurant is a worthy ambassador of the famous Japanese chain which now has branches worldwide. Talented chef Ken Sato presides over three different dining areas (sushi bar, Teppan Yaki, Shabu-Shabu). The superlative quality of the fish and shellfish in the local markets is a source of delight to Japanese chefs in Madrid, and allows them to create exquisite sushi, red tuna sashimi and Mediterranean-prawn tempura. An unforgettable experience, even though it is an expensive one.

## Pedro Larumbe (39)
### Serrano 61, 28001 ☎ (91) 575 11 12 ➡ (91) 576 60 19

Ⓜ *Rubén Darío, Núñez de Balboa* **Creative cuisine** ●●●● ▭ ◯ *Mon.–Fri. 1.30–4pm, 9pm–midnight; Sat. 9pm–midnight; closed public holidays*

Pedro Larumbe, the Navarrese chef who used to preside over the kitchen at the Cabo Mayor ➡ 64, now has his own restaurant, with his own name. The three dining rooms (the stunning Patio Andaluz, the Salón Pompeyano and the Salón Fundador) have retained the *belle époque* interior of the former headquarters of *ABC & Blanco y Negro* ➡ 130. The cuisine is appropriately *fin de siècle* too: warm lobster salad with almond mayonnaise or casserole of *kokotxas* (hake cheeks). The wine list is good, if still on the young side.

## Berceo (40)
### Hotel Villa Magna, Paseo de la Castellana 22, 28046
### ☎ (91) 576 75 00 ➡ (91) 575 22 86

Ⓜ *Rubén Darío* **French cooking, fish and shellfish** ●●●●● ▭ ◯ *daily 1–4pm, 8.30pm–midnight* ✚ 🌿

The Hyatt chain chose Jacques le Divellec to relaunch the Berceo, at the Hotel Villa Magna, making it one of the most attractive dining venues in Madrid. Decked out in wood, deep-blue fabrics and beautiful Chinese lamps, its magnificent banquet rooms have breathtaking views of the city. Second-in-command, Thierry Buffeteau, has embraced the challenge of creating a seafood-based, French-style cuisine in a city renowned for its fish and shellfish. Since his arrival in 1996 the restaurant has developed innovative dishes such as oven-baked mullet with eggplant and pine-nut ravioli and a julienne of crisp chives.

## Not forgetting

■ **La Giralda III (41)** Maldonado 4, 28006 ☎ (91) 577 77 62 ●●●
*Fried fish and Andalusian dishes served up in a relaxed décor. Cuisine similar to that of nearby Giralda I (Claudio Coello 24): fluffy rice with clams or hake in sherry.*

The Pedro Larumbe with its stately entrance hall, sophisticated Salón Fundador and banqueting area, La Redacción.

39

39

40

40

## In the area

The three most desirable neighborhoods – Salamanca, Chamberí and Chamartín – converge on the verdant Plaza del Doctor Marañón. The area combines noisy thoroughfares and peaceful oases, such as the area around the Museo Nacional de Ciencias Naturales, or the tiny garden of

# ➡ Where to eat

## Zalacaín (42)
**Álvarez de Baena 4, 28006 ☎ (91) 561 48 40 ➡ (91) 561 47 32**

Ⓜ *Rubén Darío* **Haute cuisine** ●●●●● ▢ Ⓞ *Mon.–Fri. 1.30–3.45pm, 9–11.45pm; Sat. 9–11.45pm; closed Easter week, August, public holidays*

Since the Zalacaín opened in 1974 it has been the undisputed leader among top restaurants in Madrid. Although in its early days it cut a radical figure in what was then a traditional field, chef Benjamín Urdiaín's cuisine is today regarded as classic. The interior is reminiscent of a rich 19th-century bourgeois residence, the service is impeccable, and the intelligent wine advice of Custodio Zamarra is a bonus. Hake sprinkled with thyme, warm salad of young pigeon and foie gras, turbot on a soubise of wild mushrooms and herb butter, crunchy chocolate and warm pineapple desert – each dish is presented with care. The new veranda is a pleasant addition.

## El Bodegón (43)
**Pinar 15, 28006 ☎ (91) 562 88 44 / (91) 562 31 37 ➡ (91) 562 97 25**

Ⓜ *Rubén Darío* **Modern Basque cuisine** ●●●● ▢ Ⓞ *Mon.–Fri. 1.30–4pm, 9pm–midnight; Sat. 9pm–midnight; closed public holidays, August* Ⓨ

The elegant yet simple cuisine of Hilario Arbelaitz is interpreted admirably in Madrid by chef Jose Machado. The modern paintings of proprietor Plácido Arango, one of Spain's great collectors, are a treat, while the menu offers a mouthwatering feast for the palate. Snout of Zuberoa veal, soft-boiled eggs on pickled vegetables, oven-baked hake with red pepper coulis or mille feuille with creamed rice and cinnamon ice-cream are artistic masterpieces.

## Belagua (44)
**Hotel Santo Mauro, Zurbano 36, 28010**
**☎ (91) 319 69 00 ➡ (91) 308 54 77**

Ⓜ *Alonso Martínez* **Modern Basque-Navarran cuisine** ●●●●● ▢
Ⓞ *Mon.–Sat. 1.30–3.30pm, 8.30–11pm; closed Easter week, public holidays* ✪
➡ 68

A magnificent town-house interior ➡ 22 with postmodern touches. The cuisine varies with chefs. Several special dishes are worth a mention: foie gras sautéd with celery and redcurrants, partridge *en escabeche* (marinated in vinegar with bay leaves) and veal snout with fried chickpeas. In summer the restaurant opens its pleasant terrace. A word of caution: prices are steep.

## Not forgetting

■ **Vatel (45)** Rafael Calvo 40, 28010 ☎ (91) 310 00 74 ●● *A bistro with small, cramped tables that offers good, inexpensive, Spanish-influenced modern cuisine. Try the grilled squid with beans, or stuffed cabbage with partridge and wild mushrooms. For regulars, there is a chance to become a member of the* Clan de Amigos del Restaurante Vatel.

the Museo Sorolla. ■ Where to stay
➡ 22 ➡ 26 ➡ 28 ■ After dark ➡ 68
➡ 70 ■ What to see ➡ 106

43

44

The gardens of the Santo
Mauro (left) provide the
Belagua with a superb summer
setting. At tables under the
white pergola you can have a
full meal, while on the terrace
you can sample items from the
*pica pica* menu (tapas ➡ 70).

45

43

44

To the east, Glorieta Cuatro Caminos, once a working-class neighborhood, is now home to the middle classes. To the west, the university district is now surrounded by a new business zone.

■ Where to stay ➡ 28 ■ After dark ➡ 82 ■ What to see ➡ 102

 # Where to eat

## Las Cuatro Estaciones (46)
### Paseo San Francisco de Sales 41, 28003
### ☎ (91) 553 63 05 ➡ (91) 553 32 98

Ⓜ *Guzmán el Bueno* **Creative gourmet cuisine** ●●●● ▣ Ⓥ *June–Sep: Mon.–Fri. 1.30–4pm, 9pm–midnight; Oct.–May: Mon.–Fri. 1.30–4pm, 9pm–midnight, Sat. 9pm–midnight; closed Jan. 1, Easter week, August*

Francisco Arias reigns over this modern, flower-decked dining space. Though it opened in 1981, the somber colors give it the air of a 1970s disco, but dancing is far from the thoughts of the diners as they tuck into some of the best food in Madrid, served up by young Francisco Vicente. From ravioli with asparagus to bull's tail with breadcrumbs and sautéed potatoes, or cod cased in pastry, the choice is wide-ranging and imaginative. Impeccable service at all times.

## Las Batuecas (47)
### Avenida Reina Victoria 17, 28003 ☎ (91) 554 04 52

Ⓜ *Guzmán el Bueno, Cuatro Caminos* **Popular Spanish cuisine** ●● ▣ Ⓥ *Mon.–Fri. 1–4pm, 9pm–midnight; Sat. 1–4pm*

The building and its interior are unremarkable, but the wholesome and unpretentious cuisine are certainly moteworthy. This *casa de comidas* (literally, 'meal house') has proved itself time and again. Las Batuecas opened its doors in 1954 and has survived by virtue of its above-average *comidas* – a culinary genre that, sadly, is becoming increasingly rare. The clientele remains faithful from one generation to the next, dining out here on home cooking at low prices: fried whiting, squid in their ink, omelette with potatoes (*tortilla española*) or asparagus accompanied by *callos* (tripe) *a la madrileña*. A first-class eatery.

## San Mamés (48)
### Bravo Murillo 88, 28003 ☎ (91) 534 50 65

Ⓜ *Cuatro Caminos* **Popular Spanish cuisine** ●●● ▣ Ⓥ *Mon.–Fri. 1.30–4pm, 8.30–11pm; Sat. 2.30–4pm; closed public holidays, August*

Nine tables are crammed into two small rooms decorated with multi-colored *azulejos* (ceramic tiles): signs that this is a good, honest *tasca* ➡ 36. Santiago García, however, is not content with serving up basic *tasca* cuisine. Occasionally too grand (take the fillet with duck liver, for example), the cooking is perfect when it relies on regional recipes: hotpot of haricot beans, black pudding and chorizo from Ávila, or sautéed meadow mushrooms and tripe *a la madrileña*.

### Not forgetting
■ **Sal Gorda (49)** Beatríz de Bobadilla 9, 28040 ☎ (91) 553 95 06 ●
*The dining area resembles a bourgeois dining room and the cuisine is suitably in keeping: superb menestra of fresh vegetables, excellent roast beef, bacalao ajoarriero (salt cod with garlic) and apple tart. Service is attentive, and the prices reasonable.*

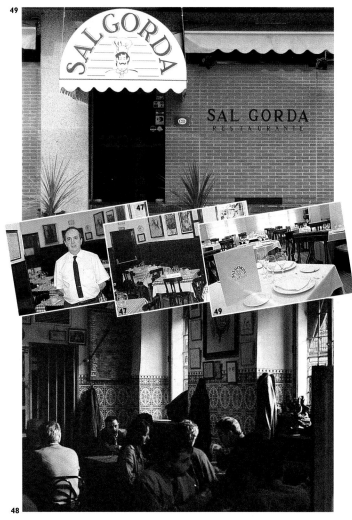

This immense ministerial complex, begun in the 1930s and completed under General Franco, together with the Azca commercial complex, its contemporary equivalent, form the hub of the modern city's expansion. The 'Manhattan of Madrid', this second city center is where the

# Where to eat

### O'Pazo (50)
**Reina Mercedes 20, 28020 ☎ (91) 533 23 33 ➠ (91) 554 90 72**

Ⓜ *Nuevos Ministerios, Alvarado* **Fish and seafood** ●●●● ▭ Ⓢ *Mon.–Sat. 1–4pm, 8.30pm–midnight; closed in August*

Evaristo García – a fishmonger in his youth and now a big name in Spain's upmarket fish trade – supplies the best restaurants in the land. In this English-style dining room, one corner of which is a library, he is in his element. Chef Francisco Monje prepares simple, perfectly cooked fish and shellfish. The oven-baked turbot with olive oil and vinegar is exquisite.

### Goizeko Kabi (51)
**Comandante Zorita 37, 28020 ☎ (91) 533 01 85 ➠ (91) 533 02 14**

Ⓜ *Alvarado* **Basque cuisine** ●●●● ▭ Ⓢ *June 16–Sep. 15: Mon.–Fri. 1.30–4pm, 8.30–midnight, Sat. 8.30pm–midnight; Sep.16–June 15: Mon.–Sat. 1.30–4pm, 8.30pm–midnight*

The Madrid branch of the famous Bilbao restaurant. The squid with onions, red meat, fried hake or woodcock roasted in Jesús Santos' old brandy are in the best Biscay tradition. English-style décor, but a small room. Book in advance.

### Gaztelupe (52)
**Comandante Zorita 32, 28020 ☎ (91) 534 90 28 ➠ (91) 554 65 66**

Ⓜ *Nuevos Ministerios, Estrechos* **Rotisserie, Basque specialties** ●●● ▭ Ⓢ *June 16–Sep. 15: Mon.–Sat. 1.30–4pm, 8.30pm–midnight, Sun. 1.30–4pm; Sep.16–June 15: Mon.–Sat. 1.30–4pm, 8.30pm–midnight*

The emphasis here is on the spectacular – or, if you like, 'Hollywood' – version of the popular Biscay inns, with all the expected classics of the genre: tender kidney beans from Tolosa, *zancarrón* (ragout) of veal, *marmitako* (a soup of tuna, potatoes and green peppers), and rice pudding. Very good wines.

### Babel (53)
**Alonso Cano 60, 28003 ☎ (91) 553 08 27**

Ⓜ *Ríos Rosas* **Armenian specialties, grilled meats** ●●● ▭ Ⓢ *Mon.–Fri. 1.30–4pm, 8.30pm–midnight; Sat. 8.30pm–midnight; closed Aug. 15–31*

The regulars know what to expect with Armik Hamparzoumian: perfect roasts of Galician beef, which have made this one of Madrid's best meat-eating establishments, and exotic hors d'oeuvres, such as the tender Armenian-style eggplants. Good red wines.

## Not forgetting

■ **Da Nicola (54)** Orense 4, 28020 ☎ (91) 553 77 53 ● *Huge underground premises offering good, authentic Italian cuisine at low prices.*
■ **Alborán (55)** Ponzano 39, 28003 ☎ (91) 399 21 50 ●● *A tiny dining room in which to enjoy good Andalusian seafood.*

multinational corporations are
located. ■ After dark ➡ 86
■ What to see ➡ 108

O'Pazo (above) is among fish and
seafood restaurants that have earned
Madrid its gastronomic reputation.
Though situated at the center of the
Iberian peninsula, nearly 200 miles
from the nearest sea, Madrid is
considered by seafood aficionados to
be the best 'port' in the country.

## In the area

From 1930 until 1970 this was an inner suburb consisting of *colonias*, or small developments of detached houses. Despite being engulfed by the city, these still survive, lending the area a touch of greenery and an air of calm. ■ Where to stay ➡ 32 ■ After dark ➡ 74

# Where to eat

### Príncipe y Serrano (56)
**Serrano 240, 28016 ☎ (91) 458 62 31 ➡ (91) 458 86 76**

Ⓜ *Concha Espina, Colombia* **Modern Castilian cuisine** ●●● ☐ Ⓞ *Mon.–Fri. 2–4pm, 9pm–midnight; Sat. 9pm–midnight; closed in August* ✖

The view of lawns and flower beds, seen through the restaurant's bay window, make it difficult to believe that you are dining in central Madrid. Service is attentive, the setting classic and luxurious, and yet Príncipe y Serrano is still affordable, thanks to intelligent management by Salvador Gallego's two daughters. Gallego, the 'guru' of haute cuisine in the Sierra of Madrid, keeps a discreet eye on this, the second of his family establishments. The cuisine is simple yet sophisticated, – try the *txangurro* (spider crab cocktail), or boned oxtail in flaky pastry. The cellar is interesting, with some very good and unusual wines, such as Veigadares, a vat-fermented white wine from Galicia.

### Casa Benigna (57)
**Benigno Soto 9, 28002 ☎ (91) 413 33 56 ➡ (91) 416 93 57**

Ⓜ *Concha Espina* **Mediterranean cuisine and Scandinavian specialties** ●●● ☐ Ⓞ *daily 1.30pm–4pm, 9pm–11.30pm*

The bright colors of this simple bistro and the landscapes on the wall divert attention from the low ceiling, which might otherwise feel oppressive. Norberto Jorge (who comes from Alicante but has lived for 20 years in Norway and still commutes between Madrid and Oslo) and his partner José Luis Gutiérrez are unpretentious, but they offer some of the most exquisitely prepared dishes in town. The dual influence produces an unique menu: the hand marinated herring with horseradish contrasts with sumptuous vegetarian paellas, prawns *en papillote* and scampi *al ajillo* (in garlic mayonnaise). There is always an excellent fish of the day and the international wine list includes some interesting finds at a range of prices.

### La Atalaya (58)
**Joaquín Costa 31, 28002 ☎ (91) 562 87 45**

Ⓜ *República Argentina* **Cantabrian cuisine** ●● ☐ Ⓞ *Wed.–Sat. 1–4pm, 9pm–midnight; Mon. 1–4pm; closed public holidays and one week in August*

The walls of La Atalaya are covered with modern paintings – the owners come from Santander, the city where virtually every restaurant and bar resembles an art gallery. The atmosphere is restrained but hospitable and the cuisine comes straight from Spain's verdant north, with specialties like *maganos* (minuscule squid) prepared with onions, and fried anchovies stuffed with *piquillos*. At lunchtime, La Atalaya offers a cheap menu, based on the rustic dishes of Cantabria (the region south of the Bay of Biscay in the province of Santander). Go on a Thursday or a Saturday to savor *cocido montanés*, a hearty cabbage soup with haricot beans, sausage and black pudding.

■ What to
see ➡ 108
■ Where to
shop ➡ 142

Norberto Jorge
(left) and José
Luis Gutiérrez
(right) run Casa
Benigna, making a
formidable team,
even when
Norbert is away
keeping an eye on
the kitchen at
Sancho, his Oslo
restaurant.

57

58

## In the area

The Palacio de Congresos and the immense Santiago Barnabéu football stadium, home of Real Madrid, extend the city northward. The shops of the Castellana and of the streets running parallel rival those of the Serrano district. ■ Where to stay ➡ 30 ■ After dark ➡ 80

 # Where to eat

### El Comité (59)
**Plaza de San Amaro 8, 28020 ☎ (91) 571 87 11 ➡ (91) 435 43 27**

Ⓜ Lima **Creative gourmet cuisine** ●●● ▢ Ⓒ Mon.–Fri. 1.30–4pm, 9pm–midnight; Sat. 9pm–12.30am; closed in August

Old photos of women's charitable committees and revolutionary parties adorn the walls of this bistro. Agnès Masso and her French chef Claude Maison d'Arblay offer elegant dishes to a devoted clientele. These include monkfish with mascarpone and a red wine sauce and julienne of fried pears, followed by hazelnut Charlotte with a coffee-flavored coulis.

### La Tahona (60)
**Capitán Haya 21, 28020 ☎ (91) 555 04 41 ➡ (91) 556 62 02**

Ⓜ Cuzco **Castilian cuisine** ●● ▢ Ⓒ Mon. –Sat. 1–4pm, 9pm–midnight; Sun. 1–4pm; closed in August

Madrid has several Hollywood-style restaurants, but La Tahona, designed to resemble a basilica, is inimitable. A branch of the restaurant chain created in Aranda de Duero, and home to tender, Castilian milk-fed lamb, the place is dedicated to the glory of this traditional roast.

### Príncipe de Viana (61)
**Manuel de Falla 5, 28036 ☎ (91) 457 15 49 ➡ (91) 457 52 83**

Ⓜ Lima **Basque and Navarin cuisine** ●●●●● ▢ Ⓒ Mon.–Fri. 1.30–3.45pm, 9–11.45pm; Sat. 9–11.45pm; closed Easter week, August, public holidays

Ramón Quintanilla, the chef who trained here before launching another successful restaurant, has returned to the fold in order to maintain the highest quality of popular cuisine in the city. In this distinctive and cheerful setting, the menestra of fresh spring vegetables and oven-baked fish merit the highest culinary accolades. Attentive service.

### El Cenachero (62)
**Manuel de Falla 8, 28036 ☎ (91) 457 59 04**

Ⓜ Lima **Mediterranean cuisine** ●● ▢ Ⓒ Mon.–Fri. 1.30–4pm, 9.30pm–midnight; Sat. 9.30pm–midnight; closed in August

This kind of small, unpretentious restaurant, perfect for an intimate dinner, is rare in Madrid. El Cenachero offers the flavors of maritime Andalusia (in Malaga a cenachero is a port peddler), interpreted delicately by chef Alberto Chicote: broad beans and mangetout with magret fumé, tomatoes stuffed with crab, tuna with a compote of tomato and basil, and sea bream with oven-roasted vegetables. Exceptional quality at reasonable prices.

## Not forgetting

■ **Asador de Roa (63)** Pintor Juan Gris 5, 28039 ☎ (91) 555 39 28 ●●
Castilian cuisine. Specialties: milk-fed oven-roasted lamb and roast piglet.

■ What to see ➡ 108
■ Where to shop ➡ 142

Calle Sor
Angela de la Cruz   Plaza de Cuzco   Av. de A. Alcocer
C. Pintor Juan Gris
Calle de Huesca
Calle del General Yagüe
Plaza San Amaro
Pedro Teixeira
Pl. Manolete
Calle del General Orgaz
Palacio de Congresos y Exposiciones
Calle del General Perón   Plaza de Lima   Av. de Concha Espina
Paseo de la Castellana
Calle Doctor Fleming
Calle de Juan Ramón Jiménez
Calle Panamá
C. de Prof. Waksman
C. del Padre Damián
C. Rafael Salgado
Estadio Santiago Bernabéu
Cuzco
Lima

59

59

59

60

62

60

'…in true Spanish inns, naturally you can eat and drink, but you also enjoy what others bring to the place.'
*Abraham Bengio*

61

## In the area

The Ciudad Lineal – a model district of villas and broad, pine-shaded avenues dating from the early 1900s – has been dramatically altered by sprawling urban developments. Mayor Arturio Soria would no longer recognize his own town. Despite this, the district is still very pleasant.

# Where to eat

### Casa d'a Troya (64)
**Emiliano Barral 14, 28043 ☎ (91) 416 44 55**

Ⓜ *Avenida de La Paz* **Galician cuisine** ●●● ▭ Ⓒ *Mon.–Sat. 1.30–3.30pm, 8.30–11pm; closed July 15–Aug. 31, Christmas, public holidays*

With the exception of a fine rustic-style slate façade, the setting is unremarkable and resembles that of a restaurant in a new suburb. However, this is a high temple of Galician tradition. Pilar Vila serves octopus, *camarones* (small shrimps), hake, pork knuckle with turnip tops, and almond rice at reasonable prices, using produce sent daily from northwestern Spain. A devoted clientele: book in advance.

### La Misión (65)
**José Silva 22, 28043 ☎ (91) 519 24 63 ➠ (91) 416 26 93**

Ⓜ *Arturo Soria* 🅟 **Classic Basque cuisine** ●●● ▭ Ⓒ *Mon.–Fri. 1.30–4pm, 9pm–midnight; Sat. 9pm–midnight; closed Easter week, August* ✪

The charming décor, complete with pink stucco and exposed beams, conjures up the image of a Spanish 17th-century mission in California. Yet the cuisine at La Misión makes few concessions to new-wave Californian cuisine. Indeed it is firmly rooted in Hispanic tradition, with a heavy Basque accent. Our gastronomic recommendation: the excellent oven-baked turbot, one of the star dishes on the menu.

### Nicomedes (66)
**Moscatelar 18, 28043 ☎ (91) 388 78 28 ➠ (91) 388 78 28**

Ⓜ *Arturo Soria* **Estremaduran specialties, creative cuisine** ●●● ▭ Ⓒ *Tues.–Sat. 1–4pm, 9–11pm; Sun. 1–4pm* ✪

A modern villa with huge bay windows opening onto a flower-filled garden, the restaurant of Elena and Concha Suárez has a strong New World flavor, with 1940s jazz playing gently in the background. The cuisine is thoroughly modern, and incorporates imaginative touches from the region of Extremadura. Dishes include Iberian pork and the exquisitely soft farm cheese, *Torta del Casar*, made from ewe's milk. The service, presided over by the two sisters, is charming and friendly, and the cellar boasts most of the best 'new' Spanish wines.

### Don Víctor (67)
**Emilio Vargas 18, 2843 ☎ (91) 415 47 47 ➠ (91) 320 93 10**

Ⓜ *Arturo Soria* 🅟 **Fish, Galician cuisine** ●●●●● ▭ Ⓒ *Mon.–Fri. 1–4.30pm, 9–11pm; Sat. 9–11pm; closed in August*

Don Víctor's modern bistro is one of the few culinary options available in a new business district still badly served by restaurants. The Galician owners offer superb fish and excellent red meats roasted in a crust of coarse salt. The high quality is reflected in the check.

**65**

**65**

**64**

**66**

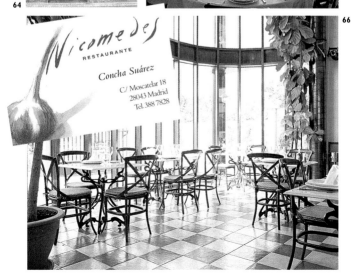

**66**

*Nicomedes*
RESTAURANTE

Concha Suárez

C/ Moscatelar 18
28043 Madrid
Tel. 388 7828

## In the area

The shaded streets of this quiet district are frequented mainly by office workers who, at various times of day, leave their work to chat or relax at the tables of the local terrace bars. ■ Where to stay ➡ 30 ➡ 32 ■ After dark ➡ 70 ➡ 80

# Where to eat

### El Olivo (68)
**General Gallegos 1, 28036 ☎ (91) 359 15 35 ➡ (91) 345 31 83**

Ⓜ *Cuzco, Plaza Castilla* **Mediterranean cuisine** ●●●● ▣ ◐ *Tues.–Sat. 1–4pm, 9pm–midnight; closed Aug. 15–30* ▆

The vocation of this olive-green restaurant is clear: virgin olive oils and Xérèz wines constitute its main culinary theme. Born in Bordeaux and raised in Andalusia, Jean-Pierre Vandelle's Franco-Spanish background produces some superb results. Don't miss the springtime specialty, lamprey in Ribera del Duero wine, or the monkfish *a la plancha* (grilled on a hot plate) with a black olive coulis.

### Aldaba (69)
**Avenida Alberto Alcocer 5, 28036 ☎ (91) 345 21 93 ➡ (91) 350 83 03**

Ⓜ *Cuzco* **Basque and Navarin cuisine** ●●●● ▣ ◐ *Mon.–Fri. 1–4pm, 9pm–midnight; Sat. 9pm–midnight; closed in August*

This intimate little restaurant was renovated by the team from Zalacaín ➡ 52, headed by José Luis Pereira. It lays on some of the best cuisine in Madrid, with an emphasis on regional and market produce: cod salad with a compote of tomatoes and spiced oil, and lasagna of monkfish and king prawns with sage.

### Cabo Mayor (70)
**Juan Ramón Jiménez 37, 28036 ☎ (91) 350 87 76 ➡ (91) 359 16 21**

Ⓜ *Cuzco* **Creative cuisine** ●●●●● ▣ ◐ *Mon.–Sat. 1–4pm, 9pm–midnight; closed Easter week, Aug. 15–31, public holidays*

The cavernous, nautical-themed interior of this restaurant is decorated in the style of a Santander farmhouse. The son and daughter of founder Victor Merino maintain the tradition of modern regional cuisine, aided by chef Carlos Barasoain's passion for spices: try the turbot with asparagus and squid or supreme of young pigeon.

### Asador Frontón (71)
**Pedro Muguruza 8, 28036 ☎ (91) 345 36 96**

Ⓜ *Cuzco* ▒ **Basque grilled meats and fish** ●●● ▣ ◐ *Mon.–Sat. 1–4pm, 9pm–midnight; Sun. 1–4pm* ▣ *Jesús y María 1, 28012 ☎ (91) 369 23 25*

Madrid is a meat-eater's paradise. With its superb Basque-style grilled meats and slabs of beef, the Frontón is the front runner in this field. The fish is equally good. A busy and noisy atmosphere. Book ahead.

## Not forgetting

■ **Sacha (72)** Juan Ramón Jimenez 37, 28036 ☎ (91) 345 59 52 ●●● *Galician cuisine served up by Pitila Hormaechea and son Sacha: clams with creamed turnips, partridge with mushrooms and rice.*
■ **Doña Paca (73)** Príncipe de Vergara 285, 28016 ☎ (91) 350 23 90 ●● *An Andalusian repertoire: diced grouper sautéed in aïoli, grilled lambs' kidneys, chocolate-and-orange fondant.*

As you go down into the Cabo Mayor (below), look up at the bronze sculptures (left) of children preparing to leap into the water to fish out the coins thrown there by passers-by – a once-familiar scene in Santander.

**La Filmoteca Española**
International movies in the original language
and special seasons.
*Cine Dore Santa Isabel 3, 28012 ☎ (91) 369 11 25*

# ➤ After dark

### Listings magazines
To check out day-to-day
cultural events:
*La Guía del Ocio,*
*weekly from news-stands.*
*¿ Que Hacer en Madrid ?,*
*free monthly from the tourist*
*office in Plaza Mayor (bilingual*
*Spanish-English).*

### Open to all
There are no private clubs in Madrid.
Some places try to discourage
customers by putting up *aforo completa*
(full) notices, but no door can resist
the determined night owl.

### 'Vamos de juerga' say
Madrileños as they prepare for a night
on the town. Not too fond of private
parties, they cram the countless bars.
They say there are more bars in one
Madrid neighborhood than in the
whole of Switzerland.

## Chocolate con churros

Follow an old city tradition and indulge in this late-night treat: long, crunchy fritters dunked in a steaming cup of thick hot chocolate.

**Chocolatería San Ginés** *Pasaje de San Ginés 5, 28013* ☎ *(91) 365 65 46*
🕐 *Oct.–May: Tue.–Thur. 7pm–10pm; Fri.–Sun. 7pm–7am; July-Aug: Tue.–Sun. 10pm–7am; June, Sep, Tue.–Thur. Midnight–7am, Fri.–Sun. 7pm–7am.*

# 49

# Nights out
## THE INSIDER'S FAVORITES

## Cultural events calendar

**May–June** Madrid City Rock Festival *Mastertrax* ☎ *(91) 304 95 17*
Madrid Dance Festival *Información del Ayuntamiento* ☎ *010*
**Summer** (Sunday Concerts by the Banda Municipal in the Parque del Retiro) *Información del Ayuntamiento* ☎ *010*
**July** Johnny Walker Music Festival *Caja de Cataluña* ☎ *(902) 38 33 33*

**July–Sep.** Summer in the City *Información del Ayuntamiento* ☎ *010*
**Sep.–Oct.** Autumn Festival *Información del Ayuntamiento* ☎ *010*
**Oct.–April** Chamber and polyphonic music concerts *Auditorio Nacional de Música* ☎ *(91) 337 01 00*
**Nov.** Jazz festival *Caja de Cataluña* ☎ *(902) 38 33 33*

## Basic facts

With the arrival of the first fine days of summer, which is always early in Madrid, the capital's inhabitants take to the streets, and re-acquaint themselves with their summer haunts. Chairs and parasols spill out onto the sidewalk as the *terrazas* re-open between April and June. This is

# After dark

### El Bulevar (1)
#### Paseo de la Castellana 37, 28046 ☎ (91) 308 51 45 / (91) 308 52 58

Ⓜ *Rubén Darío* 🕐 *May 15–Sep. 30: daily midnight–5am* 🚇 🍴 *Serrano 41–45, 28001 ☎ (91) 578 18 65 ; Paseo de la Castellana 12, 28046*

Summer visitors to Madrid are drawn inexorably to the colorful crowds filling the *terrazas* of the Castellana, the city's vital artery. Lately El Bulevar has become *the* spot to visit on a summer's night, frequented by stars and personalities such as Richard Gere, Michael Jackson and Samantha Fox. Any day of the week, however, the movers and shakers from the world of business, bullfighting, sports or showbiz come to drink here. After celebrity spotting at the Bulevar, wander down the Castellana for a drink at the terrace bars of the Bolero, Embassy or Castellana 8 ➡ 72. Here you can sample the beach-style holiday atmosphere of Madrid, complete with blaring music.

### Castellana 99 (2)
#### Paseo de la Castellana 99, 28046 ☎ (91) 337 81 46

Ⓜ *Lima* 🕐 *May–Nov.: Mon.–Thur. 7pm–3am; Fri., Sat. 7pm–4am* 🚇

Close to the Palacio de Congresos and Real Madrid's football stadium ➡ 108 is Castellana 99, a haven for those in search of peace and shade. It has a covered area for use in winter, but the chief attraction is its famous *terraza*. It is an oasis at the heart of the city's business and commercial district. The garden, complete with parasols, blinds and maritime murals, has all the trappings of a beach bar. One of its three counters serves delicious tropical cocktails, while another specializes in potent Mexican concoctions. Can cater for up to 1000 people, with seating for half this number.

### NH Santo Mauro (3)
#### Zurbano 36, 28010 ☎ (91) 319 69 00

Ⓜ *Alonso Martínez* 🕐 *May–Sep.: daily 10–3am* 🚇 🏬 *Belagua* ➡ 52

In summer the delightful garden of the NH Santo Mauro ➡ 22 is transformed into a *terraza*. One part is reserved for restaurant diners, while the other contains a bar. Shaded by magnificent chestnut trees, this is one of the most elegant and intimate places for a romantic rendezvous or for a drink with friends.

## Not forgetting

■ **Cafe de Oriente (4)** Plaza de Oriente 2, 28013 ☎ (91) 541 39 74
*In May this is one of the best* terrazas *in the city. Service is impeccable. A classic Madrileño café in a newly pedestrianized area.*
■ **El Espejo (5)** Paseo de Recoletos 31, 28004 ☎ (91) 308 23 47
*Like the famous Café Gijon further down the Paseo, the* terraza *preserves the ambience of a* belle-époque *literary café. Admire the splendid glass pavilion.*

where the *Madrileño* puts the world to rights over a coffee or cool drink, and where the visitor can taste an authentic slice of Madrid life.

## Basic facts

Various anecdotes are used to explain the origin of tapas. One theory is that *tapear* – getting a bite to eat – became popular in the reign of Charles III, when in the army it became obligatory to have something to eat with a drink in order to 'moderate' the effect of the alcohol.

# After dark

## José Luis (6)
### Serrano 89-91, 28006 ☎ (91) 563 09 58

Ⓜ *Rubén Darío* 🌐 🕐 *daily 9–1am* 🍴 🍸 ↔ *Paseo de la Habana 4, 28036 ☎ (91) 562 75 96; Paseo San Francisco de Sales 14-16, 28003 ☎ (91) 442 67 90; Rafael Salgado 11, 28036 ☎ (91) 458 80 28*

For years now, the tapas served up at José Luis have been an unmissable treat come snack-time. When you don't feel up to a full-blown meal and are looking for a relaxed atmosphere, there is always a José Luis nearby. The four branches in Madrid tend to be permanently packed, proof of the quality of the *pinchos* (literally, 'little pieces of something'), which are both varied and copious. Sirloin, hake, crab salad, fritters, salmon or potato *tortillas* are all popular, but the list is endless.

## Handicap (7)
### General Oráa 56, 28006 ☎ (91) 562 21 59

Ⓜ *Diego de León, Ruinas* 🕐 *Mon.–Sat. 1–4pm, 8pm–1am; closed public holidays, August* 🍴

The owner was a dancer at the Paris Lido in the 1950s, has performed for the Queen of England and was a triumph at Las Vegas. A fan of French refinement, his restaurant resembles a tiny Parisian bistro. Yet this is not to say that Juan Contreras has turned his back on Spain when it comes to culinary matters, for it was he who introduced to Madrid those tiny baguettes, called *bocadillos* (then later *pulgas*), which serve as a base for smoked meats, pâtés, black pudding or sirloin steak with Dijon mustard. His 'astronaut potatoes' (fried potatoes with scrambled eggs)

Another, more simple, explanation is that to *tapear* is a natural urge for the Spanish.

and *Kung-fu* (marinaded tuna with mayonnaise and vinaigrette) have been a resounding success. The cramped premises can be a problem at busy times, but this is no reason to miss out on the experience.

## Punto Cero (8)
### Serrano 93, 28006
### ☎ (91) 561 27 89

M *Rubén Darío, Avenida América* 🕓
daily 7–2am 🔲 🌟

A shopping street, a nearby business school, a pleasant owner and a wide range of *pinchos*, both hot and cold: all this explains why the Punto Cerro is full at 9pm every evening. Here, a glass of wine becomes a reason to *tapear*, which later on becomes an excuse for a full-blown meal. Outdoor seating between April and September – sometimes later – when the crowded *terraza* is noisy, but convivial.

## Not forgetting

■ **Cervecería Alemana (9)** Plaza Santa Ana ☎ (91) 429 70 33
*To tapear in this bar, or in the next-door Cervecería Santa Ana or Naturbier is one of the delights of Madrid.*
■ **La Daniela (10)** General Pardiñas 21, 28028 ☎ (91) 575 23 29
*An authentic Spanish taberna serving excellent tapas: stuffed olives, bread rubbed with garlic or topped with fresh tomato.*
■ **Las Cumbres (11)** Avenida Alberto Alcocer 32, 28036
☎ (91) 458 76 92 *To be sampled seated or at the bar: Jabugo (cured harh) oxtail, cheese, home-made fritters, squid, lettuce hearts with anchovies. A little corner of Andalucía!*

## Basic facts

Every day of the week from about 10pm in the evening, when the tapas hour is over, hundreds of places open their doors to those wanting to *ir copas* (have a drink) and listen to some music. This is the time of the night when the *Madrileños* meet up with friends and launch into

# After dark

### Cock (12)
**Reina 16, 28004 ☎ (91) 532 28 26**

Ⓜ *Gran Vía, Banco de España* 🕐 *Mon.–Thur. 7pm–3am, Fri., Sat. 7pm–4am* ● *950 Ptas* ▣

This cocktail bar never disappoints. This is partly due to its charming surroundings – the high ceiling and old oak furniture that characterize this elegant 1920s interior. The key to its success is also the *mojitos* and other delicious cocktails that can be sampled here. It has a mixed clientele from politicians to actors of stage and screen.

### Honky-Tonk (13)
**Covarrubias 24, 28010 ☎ (91) 445 68 86 ➠ (91) 445 68 86**

Ⓜ *Bilbao, Alonso Martínez* 🕐 *daily 9pm–5am* ● *800 Ptas–900 Ptas* ▣ 🎵 *Sun.–Fri. after midnight, rock, blues, fusion*

After nine years as on of the city's top venues, the Honky Tonk is still one of the best disco-bars in Madrid. Its formula: good cocktails and other drinks, live bands and exhibitions of photos and paintings. Its program satisfies lovers of country music, swing, jazz, rock or blues, and also features magicians and one-person shows. It attracts a regular crowd of sports personalities, actors and night owls, between the ages of 18 and 45.

### El Viso Madrid (14)
**Juan Bravo 31, 28006 ☎ (91) 562 23 79 ➠ (91) 562 23 79**

Ⓜ *Diego de Léon* 🕐 *daily 9pm–5am* ● *900 Ptas* ▣ 🎵 *Wed. 10.30pm* ◉ ✖

One of the latest bars to hit the scene. It was bought recently by the owners of the El Viso terrace bar, and the regular clientele followed. It is known less for its hi-tech décor than for the animated crowds jamming its entrance. Upstairs, there is a quiet area for chatting. The ground level is the place to parade or people-watch, and you can let your hair down on the downstairs dance floor.

### Gayarre (15)
**Paseo de la Castellana 118, 28046 ☎ (91) 564 25 15**

Ⓜ *Nuevos Ministerios* 🕐 *Mon.–Thur. 6pm–3am; Fri., Sat. 6pm–4am* ● *1000 Ptas* ▣

This former cinema opened as a bar in 1992. The spacious premises are decorated with bowls of fruit and rustic kitchen utensils and the candlelight and gentle background music combine to create an atmosphere that is popular with the over-35s. Twice a week, but never the same day, a surprise buffet is served up free of charge.

## Not forgetting

■ **Castellana 8 (16)** Paseo de la Castellana 8, 28046 ☎ (91) 431 30 54 *A warm welcome and intimate ambience in this bar.*

animated conversations,
setting the world to rights.

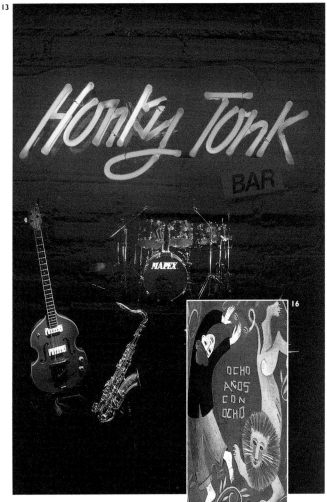

## Basic facts

When it comes to classical music, Spain is known more for its opera than for its symphonic orchestras. Nowadays, however, the choice during the season (October to June) is seemingly limitless. Concerts are held almost daily, either in the capital's main concert halls or in more unusual

# After dark

### Auditorio Nacional de Música (17)
**Príncipe de Vergara 146, 28002 ☎ (91) 337 01 00**

M *Cruz del Rayo* ◯ **Concerts** *7.30pm; 10.30pm* **Ibermúsica** ☎ *(91) 359 09 64* **Information** *daily 8am–10pm* **Box office** *Mon. 5–7pm, Tue.–Fri. 10am–5pm, Sat. 11am–1pm (for some concerts 100 tickets are on sale 1 hr before the show)* ● *prices vary* ▣ ▣

Founded in 1988, the auditorium contains two halls, one for symphonic music and the other for chamber music, with 2200 and 700 seats respectively. In the former, which is almost rectangular in shape, the ceiling has been designed to achieve maximum acoustic effect, and to allow different sections of the orchestra to be heard more precisely. The semi-circular chamber hall is designed to maintain proximity between orchestra and audience. The National Auditorium is home to the Spanish National Orchestra (the *Orquestra Nacional de España*, or ONE) and its associated choir, who play here from October to June. In tandem, the group Ibermúsica organizes the *Orchestras del Mundo* between October and May, featuring major international orchestras. Though in theory reserved for season-ticket holders, some of the upmarket hotels should be able to procure tickets. Elsewhere in the capital, the *Pro-Música* cycle and programs at the Polytechnic, Complutense and Autónoma universities are usually of interest. Finally, the concerts organized by the *Orquestra Nacional de España* and the *Liceo de Cámara* between October and June offer music lovers of all types the opportunity to enjoy both chamber and polyphonic music.

### Fundación Juan March (18)
**Castelló 77, 28006 ☎ (91) 435 42 40 ➡ (91) 576 34 20**

M *Núñez de Balboa* ◯ *Sep.–June : Mon.–Sat. 10am–2pm, 5.30–9pm; Sun., public holidays 10am–2pm* ● *free*

Renowned for its exhibitions of contemporary art, the Fundación Juan March, one of the leading cultural centers in the city, also hosts numerous chamber music concerts.

### Círculo de Bellas Artes (19)
**Marqués de Casa Riera 2, 28014 ☎ (91) 531 77 00**

M *Banco de España* ◯ **Exhibitions** *Mon.–Fri. 5–9pm; Sat. 11am–2pm, 5–9pm; Sun. 11am–2pm* ● *100 Ptas* **Movies, theater, concerts** *telephone or see Minerva for details* ● *prices vary*

This multifunctional cultural institution offers a literary café, exhibition spaces, an arts cinema, workshops and conferences, plays and top-notch concerts. Ask for a program.

## Not forgetting

■ **Teatro Monumental (20)** Atocha 65, 28012 ☎ (91) 429 81 19
*Home of the Orchestra and Choir for Spanish Radio and Television (OCTRVE). Also used by the Orchestra and Choir of the Comunidad de Madrid.*

venues. Check the programs of the major museums, for instance, as they occasionally host classical concerts.

18

17

18

## Basic facts

Taking into consideration all the national, municipal, private and public venues in the capital, Madrid is home to more than 30 different theaters. This means that it is possible to take in a first-rate production every evening. The repertoire is sufficiently wide-ranging to accommodate all

# After dark

## Teatro María Guerrero (21)
### Tamayo y Baus 4, 28004 ☎ (91) 310 29 49 ➠ (91) 319 38 36

Ⓜ Chueca, Colón ☯ **Performances** Sep.–July: Tue.–Sat. from 8pm, Sun. from 7pm **Box office** Tue.–Sat. 11.30am–1.30pm, 5–8pm ● 1650 Ptas–2600 Ptas
▭ ▣

Inaugurated in 1885 as the Teatro de la Princesa, this building is one of the best examples in Madrid of a 19th-century wrought-iron structure. The classical façade conceals a neo-Mudéjar theater which can accommodate a large audience. When it was purchased by the Spanish State, the theater was renamed Teatro María Guerrero, after the great Spanish actress who performed here for many years in the early part of this century. It is now home to Spain's Centro Dramático Nacional. The program covers the different trends in international and contemporary Spanish drama. The theater basement has a café that is quiet and friendly, frequented by both actors and theatergoers.

## Teatro Español (22)
### Príncipe 25, 28012 ☎ (91) 429 62 97 ➠ (91) 429 62 50

Ⓜ Sevilla ☯ **Performances** Tue.–Thur. 7pm; Fri., Sat. 7pm, 8.30pm **Box office** daily 11.30am–1.30pm, 5–8pm ● up to 2200 Ptas ▭ ▣

One of the oldest theaters in Europe, the Teatro Español is, with the María Guerrero, one of the most important theaters in the city. It was inaugurated as an open-air theater in 1583, and was known as the Corral de La Pacheca, or Corral del Príncipe. In 1745 it was given a roof, and was renamed Teatro del Príncipe. In 1849 it became the Teatro Español, and many of the new Romantic plays were premiered here. It became a municipal theater in 1975. In 1980 it was enlarged to accommodate 763 spectators. The program features contemporary Spanish works.

## Teatro de la Comedia (23)
### Príncipe 14, 28012 ☎ (91) 521 49 31 ➠ (91) 522 46 90

Ⓜ Sol ☯ **Performances** Sep.–June: Mon., Tue., Thur.–Sat. 8pm; Sun. 7pm **Box office** daily 11.30am–1.30pm, 5–6pm ▭ ● 1300 Ptas; Thur. –50% ▣

Housed in a 19th-century building, the Teatro de la Comedia is the home of Spain's Compañía Nacional de Teatro Clásico. This was created in order to fill a gap in the city's theater program – that of a sorely needed classical repertoire. As a result, since 1985 works by Spanish Golden Age authors such as Calderón de la Barca, Lope de Vega and Tirso de Molina have been resurrected in Madrid, and performed before the 619 spectators that the Teatro de la Comedia can accommodate.

## Not forgetting

■ **Teatro de Bellas Artes (19)** Marqués de Casa Riera 2, 28014 ☎ (91) 532 44 37 *A theater linked to the Círculo de Bellas Artes* ➠ *74. Run by director José Tamayo, it reflects both his personality and that of his troupe, the Campañía Lope de Vega, which performs also in major theaters around the country. A repertoire of Spanish authors.* ■ **Teatro Nuevo Apolo (24)** Plaza Tirso de Molina 1, 28012 ☎ (91) 429 52 38 *Popular shows and musicals.*

tastes, from the traditional to the avant-garde.

23

23

*Luces de Bohemia* by Don Ramón del Valle Inclán, directed by José Tamayo at the Teatro de Bellas Artes.

19

21

22

23

## Basic facts

The *zarzuela* is a form of light opera unique to Spain and not to be missed. Like other Mediterranean countries, Spain has a strong vocal tradition and some superb singers. It excels equally at dance with the world-class Ballet Nacional de España.

# After dark

### Teatro de la Zarzuela (25)
**Jovellanos 4, 28014 ☎ (91) 524 54 00 ➡ (91) 429 71 57**

Ⓜ *Banco de España, Sevilla* Ⓢ *Ballet Sep.–Oct. : Mon.–Sun. 8pm* ● *800 Ptas–3,500 Ptas* **Zarzuela** *Nov.–July : Mon.–Sun. 8pm* ● *1200 Ptas–4000 Ptas* **Opera** *ask for a program* ● *1200 Ptas–13,200 Ptas* **Box office** *daily noon–6pm; performance days noon–8pm* ▢ Ⓨ

Since 1964 the Teatro de la Zarzuela has hosted an annual festival of opera, *zarzuela* (Spanish operetta) and ballet. The opera and *zarzuela* season consists of a dozen or so carefully selected works, among them at least one little-known piece. The Spanish dance tradition is upheld by the Ballet Nacional de España, which since 1978 has mounted high-quality shows over a short, one-month season. Contemporary ballets are interpreted by the Compañía Nacional de Danza (National Dance Company). It performs here for an average of one month per year, depending on its touring program. Since October 1997 many of the *bel canto* operas have returned to the Teatro Real ➡ 92, Madrid's official opera house. Renovation of the latter has transformed it into a world-class opera venue. The Teatro de la Zarzuela and the Teatro Real are the twin beacons of opera in Spain.

### Teatro Albéniz (26)
**Paz 11, 28012 ☎ (91) 522 02 00 ➡ (91) 522 75 84**

Ⓜ *Sol* Ⓢ *Performances Mon.–Sat. 8.30pm; Sun. 7pm; closed July 15–Aug. 15* **Box office** *daily 11.30am–1pm, 5.30–9pm* ● *1500 Ptas–2200 Ptas* ▢ Ⓓ

This tiny theater hosts a varied program of theater, dance and music organized by the regional government within the context of the Madrid festivals. During the Mozart Festival in May and June, a whole range of operas and other works by the famous composer are performed.

### Teatro Calderón (27)
**Atocha 18, 28012 ☎ (91) 369 14 34**

Ⓜ *Tirso de Molina* Ⓢ *Performances Sep.–July: Mon.–Fri. 8pm; Sat. 7pm, 11pm; Sun. 7.30pm* **Box office** *daily 11am–2pm, 4–10pm* ● *3000 Ptas–7500 Ptas* ▢ Ⓓ

Bought by the municipality in 1996, this theater hosts a program of events ranging from popular *zarzuelas* (in the summer) to well-known operas (during the rest of the year). Its repertoire features popular operas such as *Madama Butterfly* or *La Bohème*, Spanish operettas such as *Bohemios* or *La Alegría de la Huerta* and moving recitals by Isabel Pantoja.

## Not forgetting

■ **Centro Cultural de la Villa (28)** Plaza de Colón, 28001
☎ (91) 575 60 80
*Hidden beneath the monument to Columbus and the fountains of this square ➡ 104 is a remarkable purpose-built cultural center which, from time to time, hosts zarzuela and flamenco shows ➡ 80. See program for details.*

**27**

**25**

**25**

**28**

## Basic facts

Nearly every performing company in Spain ends its tour by coming to Madrid, including the country's best flamenco and *sevillana* shows. Seize an opportunity to spend an evening in a *tablao* (literally, 'stage') or *sala rociera*. In a *tablao*, or Andaluz bar, you will be applauding the footwork of

# After dark

### Corral de la Morería (29)
**Morería 17, 28005 ☎ (91) 365 84 46**

Ⓜ *Latina, Opera* 🕐 *daily from 9pm* **Performance** *10.45pm–2am* ● **Dinner performance** *10,000 Ptas* **Bar performance** *4000 Ptas* ▣

Hidden away at the Corral de la Morería in the Castilian district of Las Vistillas is one of the more surprising flamenco *tablaos*, both for its long tradition and for the purity of its performance. The ballet that founded the place in 1956 included famous dancers such as Pastora Imperio. Other great names, such as Antonio Gades, La Chunga and Lucero Tena, followed. The star of the moment is Blanca del Rey. The small room is ideally suited to the smouldering intimacy of a flamenco dance, while the Castilian-style décor is sober and elegant.

### Café de Chinitas (30)
**Torija 7, 28013 ☎ (91) 559 51 35**

Ⓜ *Santo Domingo* 🕐 *Mon.–Sat. dinner served from 9pm* **Performance** *10.30pm–2am* ● **Dinner performance** *9500 Ptas* **Bar performance** *from 300 Ptas* ▣

Art and history interweave to great effect in this 17th-century palace, now renovated and decorated with valuable paintings, sculptures in bronze and marble, bullfighting memorabilia and a superb collection of Manila shawls ➡ 128. The famous dancer La Chunga appeared at its opening in 1969. Since then, flamenco stars such as Manuela Vargas, Enrique Morente, José Mercé and Pastora Vega have performed here.

### Al Andalus (31)
**Capitán Haya 19, 28020 ☎ (91) 556 14 39**

Ⓜ *Cuzco* 🕐 *Mon.–Sat. 11pm–6am; closed 15 days from July to August* ● *Mon.–Wed. 2000 Ptas; Thur.–Sat. 3000 Ptas* ▣

Al Andalus is more of a *sala rociera* than a *tablao,* where you can dance passionate *sevillanas* or athletic rumbas with the *rocieros*. It is impossible to stay seated. Al Andalus transports you to the lively streets of Andalusia with the bar's southern *mosaicos* (Andalusian tiles), white-washed balconies, flowers, roasts and the fiesta flamenca.

### Tablao de la Pacheca (32)
**Juan Ramón Jiménez 26, 28036 ☎ (91) 359 26 60**

Ⓜ *Plaza Castilla, Cuzco* 🕐 *daily 8.15pm–2am* ● **Dinner performance** *9500 Ptas–12,500 Ptas* **Bar performance** *4300 Ptas* ▣

A famous *tablao* on two levels. The ballets performed here are of the highest standard. The *bailaoras* (female dancers) are splendidly costumed in spotted dresses and colored shawls.

## Not forgetting

■ **Almonte (33)** Juan Bravo 35, 28006 ☎ (91) 563 54 04
*Somewhere to practise the* sevillana, *rumba or salsa!*

the audience; in a *sala rociera* you may find yourself joining in with the dancers on the floor.

29

29

30

29

29

30

29

You will find fewer cabarets in Madrid than any other European capital. A reason for this could be that the Spanish, who are by nature fidgety and talkative, are restless spectators. Those that do exist, however, are worth seeing. The shows are invigorating and of a high quality. Madrid

# After dark

## Berlín Cabaret (34)
**Costanilla de San Pedro 11, 28005 ☎ (91) 366 20 34**

M *La Latina* P 🕐 *Mon.–Thur. 11pm–5am; Fri., Sat. 11pm–6am performances from 1.30am* ● *1000 Ptas* 🎵

An evocation of the Prohibition era, with exotic shows, near-naked women, drag-queens, dancing, magic tricks, plenty of humor and a dose of 1930s social satire. The Berlin Cabaret is the perfect place for a drink in a unusual setting. It is not a traditional cabaret, nor a café, but a bar, dance club and meeting-place all rolled into one. In short, somewhere to be thoroughly entertained.

## Florida Park (35)
**Paseo de coches del Retiro, 28009 ☎ (91) 573 78 05**

M *Ibiza* 🕐 *Mon.–Sat. from 9pm* **Performance** *10.30pm–3am* ● **Dinner performance** *9000 Ptas* **Bar performance** *4300 Ptas* ▣ 🎵

Located right in the heart of the Parque del Retiro ➡ 98, Florida Park was for a long time the place to hear major Spanish and international artists such as Lola Flores, Chavela Vargas, Liza Minelli, Plácido Domingo and Diana Ross. Today, flamenco ➡ 80 and other types of Spanish dance music are on the program, and the orchestra is as happy to play old bolero and salsa classics as it is to play the latest tunes.

## Clamores Jazz (36)
**Albuquerque 14, 28010 ☎ (91) 445 79 38**

M *Bilbao* 🕐 *daily 7pm–3am, Sun.–Mon. dancing after 10pm* ● *500 Ptas* 🎵 *Tue.–Sat.* ● *prices vary* ▣

Jazz, country, salsa and blues are just some of the different types of live music on offer at the Clamores. Here, you can hear Ismaël Serrano, Jayme Marqués, Pedro Iturralde, Jorge Drexler, Lonnie Smith, Billy Brooks and many others. Should you wish to seize the microphone, a pianist will accompany you until the audience gives in and applauds.

## Scala Meliá (37)
**Rosario Pino 7, 280020 ☎ (91) 571 44 11**

M *Plaza Castilla* P 🕐 *Tue.–Sat. from 8.30pm* **Performances** *Tue.–Fri. 10.45pm Sat. 10.45pm–12.15am* ● **Dinner performance** *9900 Ptas* **Bar performance** *5100 Ptas* ▣ 🎵

A spectacular setting, with a skating rink, swimming pool, water cascades, bridges, floating staircases, hydraulic platforms, featuring exotic beauties, dancers, musicians and other artistes, always of a high standard. Excellent variety shows. An unusual venue that is a must for night owls.

### Not forgetting
■ **Galileo Galilei (38)** Galileo 100, 28015 ☎ (91) 534 75 57
*Café concerts. An extensive program featuring a variety of shows. Salsa evenings.*

has a selection of off-the-beaten-track venues offering everything from live concerts to exotic shows in good-humored spirit.

N ↑

Tetuán

37 Chamartín

Moncloa Aravaca

Ciudad Lineal

Río Manzanares

38 Chamberí

36

Salamanca

Centro

34

35
Retiro

Arganzuela

36

35

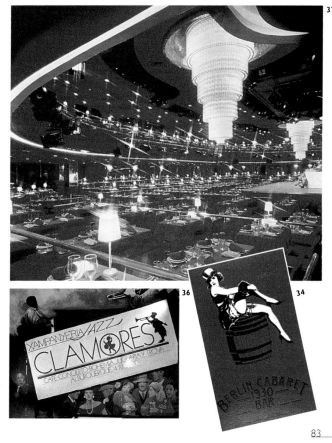

37

36

34

## Basic facts

When people talk of Madrid as the 'party capital', they are usually referring to the huge number of clubs and their one great advantage over their European counterparts: their long hours. The clientele is varied, though there are some places where the 'urban tribe' look is *de rigueur*.

# After dark

### Joy Eslava (39)
**Arenal 11, 28013 ☎ (91) 366 54 39 ➡ (91) 366 54 40**

Ⓜ *Sol* 🕐 *daily 11.30pm–6am* **Performances** *Thur.–Sun. around 2am* ● *Sun.–Wed. 1500 Ptas; Thur.–Sat. 2000 Ptas* ▣

The star of the Madrid scene, Joy Eslava is housed in a former variety theater. The interior has retained its tiered balconies, which overlook the dance floor, and its 19th-century Romantic décor, and serves as a backdrop for social gatherings, cultural events, fashion shows, movie premieres and concerts. The clientele is the most cosmopolitan of all Madrid night spots, comprising movie stars, theater actors, dancers, literary figures, politicians, TV personalities and members of Madrid's jet-set.

### Empire (40)
**Paseo de Recoletos 16, 28001 ☎ (91) 435 84 50**

Ⓜ *Colón* 🕐 *daily 11pm–5am* ● *Fri., Sat. 2000 Ptas, Sun.–Thur. 1000 Ptas* ▣

The Empire is a mix of traditional and modern, in both its clientele and its décor. It once played host to luminaries such as Gloria Estefan, Prince, Omar Shariff, Antonio Banderas, Pedro Almodóvar and Steven Seagal. It has preserved its theatrical charm, and still draws a mixed crowd. Plenty of *marcha* (ambience) and good music.

### Pachá (41)
**Barceló 11, 28004 ☎ (91) 447 01 28**

Ⓜ *Bilbao* 🕐 *Wed.–Sat. 11.30pm–6am* ● *1500 Ptas* ▣

'When you go by Pachá, don't forget to visit Madrid.' This famous saying tells you a lot about the reputation of this club with *Madrileños* and visitors alike. Attractive people, good music, and a packed dance floor – Pachá has become the late-night legend of Madrid.

### Nells (42)
**López de Hoyos 25, 28006 ☎ (91) 562 49 54**

Ⓜ *Avenida América, Cruz del Rayo* 🕐 *Tue.–Sat. midnight–6am* ● *4500 Ptas* ▣ 🍸

This small, recently opened club, with its élite clientele, is to Madrid what private clubs are to other European capitals. This is where the beautiful people meet: mostly over-25s, jackets but no ties, glamorous, well-dressed women and good music. At weekends, book a table in advance to avoid being suffocated at around 3am. On Tuesdays there is a flamenco *fiesta* ➡ 80, usually by invitation only.

## Not forgetting

■ **Palacio de Gaviria (43)** Arenal 9, 28013 ☎ (91) 526 60 69 *A gorgeous 19th-century palace hosting tea dances, disco nights and salsa evenings.*

## Basic facts

If you're still not ready to fall into bed at 7am, you're not alone. On the contrary, your profile fits perfectly with that of the Madrid night owl, and the city's numerous after hours venues await you. These stay open until midday or even later, enabling you to effect the transition from aperitif

# After dark

## Underground (44)
**Pasaje Martín de los Heros 14, 28008 ☎ (91) 388 99 72**

Ⓜ *Plaza de España* 🕒 *Thur.–Sun. 5–10.30am* ● *1500 Ptas* ▣

It is not until around 6am that the first visitors trickle into Underground. The décor is modern and the premises can accommodate up to 1600 people. There are three bars, where you can continue to drink and listen or dance to house music. The clientele is mixed, and everyone is good-humored and welcoming. An uplifting experience after a night on the town.

## Kitsch (45)
**Galileo 26, 28015 ☎ (91) 447 44 95**

Ⓜ *Argüelles* 🕒 *Fri.–Sat. 5–11am* ● *1500 Ptas* ▤

Kitsch opened up about a year ago in the old Revolver concert hall. About 1000 people can pack into the place at peak weekend hours – between 5am and 7.30am. The place is dimly-lit with an 'underground' décor and techno music. The regular clientele, boys and girls aged between 20 and 35, always seems good-looking and fashionable, even when dancing after dawn.

## Racha (46)
**Orense 18, 28020 ☎ (91) 561 02 88/(929) 04 35 59**

Ⓜ *Nuevos Ministerios* 🕒 *Thur. 6–11am; Fri., Sat. 6am–4pm* ● *1000 Ptas* ▣

A visit to Racha may be one of the most intense nights out you have in Madrid. For the first ten minutes or so, you will need to adjust to a backdrop of ear-shattering music. Stay with it, though, because Racha will surprise you. Don't be tempted to return to the light too soon. The best time to go is obviously not in the afternoon even if the open doors still beckon – but the night is still young at Racha at 7am.

## Fun Factory (47)
**Orense 24, 28020 ☎ (91) 555 96 32**

Ⓜ *Lima, Nuevos Ministerios* 🕒 *Sat., Sun. 6–11am* ● *1500 Ptas* ▣

The Fun Factory, or Cache, was a normal nightclub up until 1993, when its owners decided to open it up for a second session later on in the night. The premises are light and spacious, the music is good, and includes *bakalao* (Spanish techno). Three bars, constant activity and a mixed crowd aged between 20 and 40 years old – a lively crowd of night owls emerging from the capital's regular nightclubs ➡ 84 and still in search of fun.

## Not forgetting

■ **Roxy (48)** Orense 14, 28020 ☎ (929) 04 35 59
*The hottest night spot in Madrid. A magnet for theater and showbiz types, who continue to cavort to the rhythms of the Animadoras at 10am.*

to lunchtime appetizer with ease! These places welcome all sorts of people – including those who have just woken up.

Late-night venues is probably the wrong term – many of these places don't even *start* to liven up until well into the early morning.

**Bono museo**
You can buy a pass for the Centro Cultural Reina Sofía, the Prado and Museo Thyssen-Bornemisza at any of the three museums ● 1050 Ptas

# What to see

## Bus tours

Privately-operated buses run regularly between Palacio Real and Plaza de Colón. Take the whole tour, or get off at any stop and take the next bus.
*Madrid Vision* Avenida Manoteras 14, 28050 ☎ (91) 767 17 43
● 1600 Ptas for a panoramic tour, 2000 Ptas for one day, 2500 Ptas for two days.

# 46
# Sights
THE INSIDER'S FAVORITES

## Guided tours
*Asociación de Guías de Madrid*
Ferraz, 82-bajo derecha, 28008
☎ (91) 542 12 14 ➡ (91) 541 12 21
🕑 Mon.–Fri. 8am–7pm; Sat. 9am–1pm
● Pick your own itinerary. From 12,000 Ptas for a three-hour walking tour for up to 30 people.

## Helicopter trips
You can hire a helicopter from
*Empresa Hispanica de Aviación*
Aeropuerto de 4 Vientos, Avenida del Valle 13, 28003 ☎ (91) 553 85 01
● 162,400 Ptas for a one-hour flight, maximum 5 people

# What to see

## Palacio Real (1)
### Bailén, 28071 ☎ (91) 542 00 59 ➡ (91) 542 69 47

Ⓜ *Opera* 🕐 *Oct. 1–Mar 31: Mon.–Sat. 9.30am–5pm, Sun. 9am–2pm; Apr. 1–Sep 30: Mon.–Sat. 9am–4pm, Sun. 9am–3pm; closed on official ceremony days* ● *850 Ptas; over 65 years, students, children 350 Ptas; Wed. free* 📁 🗓 *950 Ptas* 🔌 ⊞

The Palacio Real (Royal Palace) is one of the most majestic monuments in the city. It was built on the ruins of the Alcázar (fortress) of Madrid, destroyed by fire in 1734. Completed in 1764, in the reign of Charles III (1759–88), the palace was designed by Italian architect Gianbattista Sacchetti, and construction was supervised by architects Ventura Rodríguez and Francisco Sabatini. The neoclassical structure was modified to suit the difficult terrain – a hill sloping steeply to the Manzanares river. Away from the river, on the other side of the palace, is the Plaza de Oriente. An equestrian statue of Philip II – a superb piece of 18th-century sculpture by Pietro Tacca – stands at its center.

**Inside** the palace, highlights include the Throne Room, which has a superb view of the Campo del Moro, the sumptuous Dining Room (Comedor), the Porcelain Room, the Sala Gasparini, the grand staircase (each step cut from a single block of marble), and the Chapel, which has a remarkable collection of stringed instruments. In the various rooms hang paintings by Velázquez, Goya, El Greco, Rubens and Tiepolo. The palace's collection of tapestries is the largest in Europe, and charts the development of this decorative art from its Gothic origins to the late-18th century. One of the most impressive exhibits in the palace is the Armería Real (Royal Armoury), which exhibits weaponry from the Middle Ages through to the modern day. If there is time, try to visit the Farmácia (Royal Pharmacy), which has a display of Talavera ceramic jars, and the Museo de Carruajes (Carriage Museum), which houses a collection of 18th- and 19th-century vehicles (access is via the Sabatini gardens).

**The Palace Gardens**, or Campo del Moro, are attached to the west wing of the palace. Laid out under Isabel II (1833–68), they reflect the English landscape style that was popular in Madrid at the time. Note the splendid fountains, as well as the fantastic view of the palace's west face. Access to the gardens is via a grand flight of steps; another, toward the north side, leads down to the French-style Sabatini gardens, embellished with statues and fountains. These formal gardens were laid out in the reign of Alfonso XII (1874–85).

## Not forgetting
■ **Catedral de la Almudena (2)** Mayor 90, 28007
🕐 *daily 10am–2pm, 6–8pm Work on the cathedral began in 1879. The plans were modified so many times during construction, however, that it was consecrated only in 1992.*
■ **El Viaducto (3)** Calle Bailén/Calle Segovia, 28071 *This viaduct is one of the city's marvels of civil engineering. Built in 1932 along 'rationalist' lines, it straddles the canyon-like Calle Segovia, and links the Royal Palace with the southern part of the city.*

main residence for all Spanish
monarchs, except the
present king, Juan Carlos.
■ After dark ➡ 68 ➡ 80

The State Dining
Room is one of the
palace's most
magnificent rooms.

**In the area**
This district in Old Madrid, a warren of streets and famous squares (once the setting for official ceremonies and public events) is one of the most beautiful and unspoiled areas of the city. ■ Where to stay ➡ 20 ■ Where to eat ➡ 38 ■ After dark ➡ 68 ➡ 80 ➡ 84

# What to see

## Plaza Mayor (4)

Ⓜ *Sol, La Latina*

The Plaza Mayor is the largest square in the historic center of Madrid. Its present appearance is the result of work by Juan de Villanueva (1789–1811), the architect of the Prado ➡ 96. It comprises a medieval marketplace (adjacent streets are named after confraternities and guilds), the *Casa de la Panadería* (headquarters of the bakers' guild) and the *Casa de la Carnicería* (headquarters of the butchers' guild). The square evolved into the social hub of the city, hosting public spectacles, jousts and even bullfights ➡ 100. Today its shops, restaurants and architecture draw many visitors. The front of the Casa de la Panadería is decorated with frescoes by Carlos Franco depicting the classic symbols of Madrid: allegories of water and the countryside, *majos* and *majas* (elegant 17th-century men and women), *toreros* and 'cats' (the nickname given to the *madrileños*).

## Plaza de la Villa (5)
☎ (91) 588 10 00

Ⓜ *Ópera, La Latina* 🕓 *Casa de la Villa / Casa de Cisneros Mon. 5–7pm* ● *free* 🅿

The buildings around Plaza de la Villa (Town Square) include several examples of the architectural style favored by the Hapsburgs. The *Ayuntamiento* (Town Hall) – also called the *Casa de la Villa* – is built on two levels around a patio, and flanked by pinnacle towers decorated with coats of arms. Inside, the grand staircase, the *Patio de Cristales*, the former chapel and the *Allegory of 2nd of May* (Francisco de Goya) merit close inspection. The *Casa de Cisneros*, built in 1537, is one of the finest examples of the Plateresque style (from *platero*, the Spanish word for silversmith), characterized by its intricate detail. Opposite the *Ayuntamiento* is the tower of Los Lujanes. It has two portals – one Gothic and the other, with an overreaching arch, that is typically Moorish. The statue in the center of the square represents Alvaro de Bazán, admiral of the 'invincible' Armada of Philip II (1556–98).

### Not forgetting
■ **Monasterio de las Descalzas Reales (6)** Plaza de las Descalzas Reales, 28013 ☎ (91) 542 00 59 🕓 Tue.–Sat. 10.30am–12.30pm, 4–5.30pm *A convent housing a rich collection of paintings, sculptures, tapestries and reliquaries. One of the finest Baroque collections in Spain.*
■ **Teatro Real (7)** Plaza de Oriente 5, 28013 ☎ (91) 516 06 00 *A 19th-century theater transformed into a concert hall in 1940. Following recent work, it has become a companion opera house to the Teatro Zarzuela ➡ 78.*
■ **Monasterio de la Encarnación (8)** Plaza de la Encarnación 1, 28013 ☎ (91) 542 00 59 🕓 Wed., Sat., Sun. 10.30am–12.45pm, 4–5.30pm *An Augustin convent. Parts of the cloisters are open to the public. A remarkable collection of 17th-century Madrid School paintings. An impressive and ornate reliquary.*

■ Where to
shop ➥ 126
➥ 128 ➥ 144

Map labels: Sto. Domingo, Callao, C. Encarnación, C. de Fomento, C. Jacometrezo, C. de la Bola, C. Calle de Preciados, C.San Quintín, Calle de Arrieta, Cuesta de Sto. Domingo, C. Campomanes, C. de los Ángeles, C. Veneras, Jardines Cabo Noval, Plaza de Oriente, C.Felipe V, Calle Flora, Plaza San Martín, C.Misericordia, Opera, Plaza Isabel II, C.Carlos III, C.de Vergara, C. del Arenal, Hileras, C.San Martín, Jardines Lepanto, C. de Vergara, C.Amnistía, C.Escalinata, C.las Fuentes, Calle de las, C.Bordadores, Calle Mayor, Plaza Ramales, C. Espejo, C. San Nicolás, C. Santiago, C. del Factor, Calle Mayor, Cta Plaza, Plaza Morenas, Cava San Miguel, C.de Toledo, Plaza Mayor

6

4

4

7

6

## In the area

The opening up of the Gran Vía was the first major urban project of the early 1900s. A cosmopolitan symbol of the city, it includes some beautiful 1920s architecture. ■ Where to stay ➡ 18 ➡ 20 ■ Where to eat ➡ 40 ➡ 42 ■ After dark ➡ 70 ➡ 72 ➡ 74 ➡ 76 ➡ 78

# What to see

## Gran Vía (9)

Ⓜ *Gran Vía, Callao, Plaza de España*

The Gran Vía is a broad, mile-long thoroughfare that links Plaza de Cibeles ➡ 96 with Plaza de España ➡ 102. Work was carried out in three phases, each corresponding to a different section. Along the first section, from the Plaza de Cibeles to Red de San Luis (at the intersection of Calle de Fuencarral and Calle de Hortaleza), the buildings resemble Parisian apartment blocks of the late-19th century. The Edificio Metrópolis (no. 39), located at the corner of Gran Vía and Calle de Alcalá, typifies this exuberant and theatrical style. On Calle de Alcalá (no. 42) to the left of it, is the Círculo de Bellas Artes ➡ 74, a striking building designed by architect Antonio Palacios. From the Red de San Luis the buildings resemble, on a reduced scale, the first skyscrapers of Chicago. The Compañía Telefónica building (no. 28), housing Spain's national telephone company, was the first skyscraper to be erected in Madrid, though its façade is more Madrid Baroque than avant-garde. Closing this second section of the Gran Vía are three unusual buildings: Palacio de la Prensa; Palacio de la Música; and the Callao Cinema. The brick Palacio de la Prensa (no. 46) was the fist Madrid apartment block to be given an art deco façade, revealing its debt to German Expressionism. Huge cinema posters conceal the curious façade of Palacio de la Música (no. 35), whose decorative details were inspired by the Madrid Baroque. The art deco interior of the Callao Cinema is worth seeing. The third section of the Gran Vía begins at the curved corner of the Edificio Carrión (no. 78), which now houses the Capitol Cinema (no. 41). It ends at the pared-down Edificio Coliseum (no. 78), yet another cinema. This last section is easily the most colorful part of Madrid.

## Bellas Artes de San Fernando (10)
### Alcalá 13, 28014 ☎ (91) 522 14 91

Ⓜ *Sevilla, Sol* Ⓢ **Museum** *Mon., Sat., Sun. 9am–2.30pm; Tue.–Fri. 9am–7pm* ● *Mon.–Fri. 300 Ptas; children 150 Ptas; over-65s, students, Sat., Sun. free* **Exhibitions** *Mon., Sat., Sun. 10am–2pm, Tue.–Fri. 10am–2pm, 5–8pm* ● *free* 🗗 🖥 ▦

The second most important museum in Madrid after the Prado ➡ 96. The collection includes thirteen canvases by Francisco de Goya, numerous 17th-century sculptures and paintings (Zurbarán, Murillo, Pedro de Mena, Rubens and Van Dyck), a series of Italian paintings from the 16th century (including the only Archimboldo in Spain) and a series of academic paintings from the 18th, 19th and 20th centuries.

## Not forgetting

■ **Puerta del Sol (11)** *The geographical centre of Madrid and, up until the 1950s, the scene of historic events. Statues of Mariblanca and the oso and madroño (bear and arbutus tree), which feature on the city's coat of arms. Monument dedicated to King Juan Carlos.*
■ **Plaza de las Cortes (12)** *The Chamber of Deputies (1850) is the most important building on this square. Designed by Pascual y Colomer, it has a colonnaded portico and a classical pediment.*

■ Where to
shop ➥ 126
➥ 128 ➥ 130
➥ 132

9

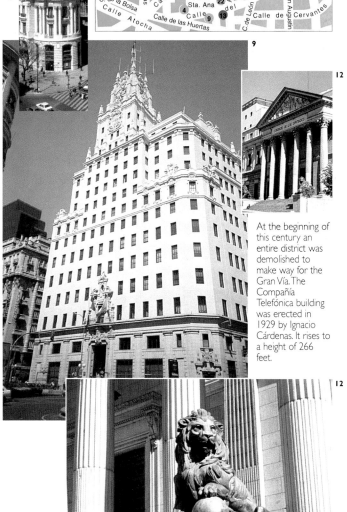

At the beginning of
this century an
entire district was
demolished to
make way for the
Gran Vía. The
Compañía
Telefónica building
was erected in
1929 by Ignacio
Cárdenas. It rises to
a height of 266
feet.

## In the area

This shady avenue is often referred to as the Paseo del Arte (literally, the 'Art Walk'), and with good reason, for it is home to Madrid's great art museums. ■ Where to stay ➡ 18 ■ Where to eat ➡ 40 ➡ 42 ■ Where to shop ➡ 138

# What to see

## Museo del Prado & Casón del Buen Retiro (13)
**Paseo del Prado, 28014 ☎ (91) 330 28 00 ➡ (91) 330 28 58**

Ⓜ *Atocha, Banco de España* 🕐 *Tue.–Sat. 9am–7pm; Sun., public holidays 9am–2pm* ● *500 Ptas; students 250 Ptas; over-65s, children free*

Designed in 1785 by Juan de Villanueva, the building houses one of the world's leading art museums. The collections (originally part of the Spanish royal art collection) cover three great schools of painting. The Spanish School numbers among its works many El Grecos, the world's largest Velázquez collection (over sixty canvases, including his most famous painting *Las Meninas*) and works by Goya (court portraits and 'dark paintings'). The glorious Italian collection includes works by Fra Angelico, Raphael and Titian. The Flemish School has some superb pieces by Bosch and Rubens. The Prado also contains around 500 sculptures of Graeco-Roman, Renaissance and Baroque origin. The nearby annexe was once the ballroom of the palace of El Casón del Buen Retiro. Now run by the National Museum of Modern Art, it contains Spanish sculptures and paintings from the 19th century.

## Museo Thyssen-Bornemisza (14)
**Paseo del Prado 8, 28014 ☎ (91) 420 39 44 ➡ (91) 420 27 80**

Ⓜ *Banco de España* 🕐 *Tue.–Sun. 10am–7pm* ● *600 Ptas; over-65s, students 350 Ptas; children free*

Since 1992 the Palacio de Villahermosa has housed the superb private collection of baron von Thyssen-Bornemisza. Over 800 works of western art are on display in the museum. Among them are *Saint Catherine of Alexandria* by Caravaggio, Venetian views by Canaletto, *Venus and Cupid* by Rubens and *Easter Morning* by Caspar David Friedrich. There is a good collection of Impressionist and post-Impressionist art, an impressive canvas by Mark Rothko, a leading American Abstract Expressionist, and an eclectic display of Soviet avant-garde works.

## Not forgetting

■ **Plaza de Cibeles (15)**
*A Castilian square designed by Ventura Rodríguez in 1775. Fountain dedicated to the goddess of nature, Cibeles.*
■ **Puerta de Alcalá (16)** Plaza de la Independencia, 28001
*Symbol of Enlightenment Madrid. A neoclassical granite gate by Francisco Sabatini (1778).*
■ **Plaza Cánovas del Castillo (17)**
*The twin sister of Cibeles, by Ventura Rodríguez (1780). Fountain dedicated to Neptune.*
■ **San Jerónimo el Real (18)** Moreto 4, 28014 ☎ (91) 420 35 78
🕐 *daily 9am–1pm, 5–8.30pm*
*Built over the ruins of a monastery. The church was erected under the Catholic Monarchs and was modified in the 19th century. Juan Carlos I was crowned here.*
■ **Museo del Ejército (19)** Méndez Núñez 1, 28014 ☎ (91) 522 89 77
🕐 *Tue.–Sat. 10am–2pm*
*An extensive military collection.*

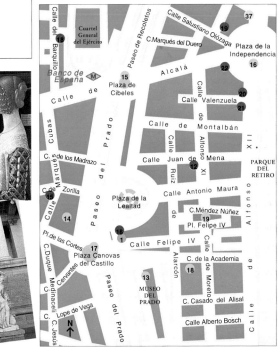

Calle Salustiano Olózaga
Calle del Barquillo
Cuartel General del Ejército
Paseo de Recoletos
C. Marqués del Duero
Plaza de la Independencia
Banco de España
Plaza de Cibeles
Alcalá
Calle Valenzuela
Calle de Montalbán
Calle de Alfonso XII
Calle Juan de Mena
Calle de los Madrazo
C. Marqués de Cubas
C. de Zorilla
Calle Ruiz
Calle Antonio Maura
Plaza de la Lealtad
C. Méndez Núñez
Pl. Felipe IV
Paseo del Prado
Pl. de las Cortes
C. Duque de Medinaceli
Cervantes
Calle Felipe IV
Plaza Canovas del Castillo
C. de la Academia
C. de Moreto
MUSEO DEL PRADO
Alarcón
C. Casado del Alisal
Lope de Vega
C. Jesús
Calle Alberto Bosch
PARQUE DEL RETIRO
N

fundación COLECCIÓN THYSSEN-BORNEMISZA

## In the area

The Glorieta (roundabout) of Charles V, known simply as Atocha, marks the city's southern perimeter. The Centro Cultural Reina Sofia completes the so-called 'Golden Triangle' bordered on its other sides by the Prado and Thyssen-Bornemisza museums.

# What to see

## Centro Cultural Reina Sofia (20)
### Santa Isabel 52, 28012 ☎ (91) 467 50 62 ➠ (91) 467 84 31

Ⓜ Atocha 🕐 Mon.–Sat. 10am–9pm; Sun. 10am–2.30pm ● 500 Ptas; students 250 Ptas; over-65s, children, Sat. afternoon, Sun. 2.30pm free 🎫 🖼 ☎ (91) 527 72 05 🏧 ♨ ▮ ▯

Designed by Francisco Sabatini in 1776, this former hospital today houses Madrid's National Museum of Contemporary Art. The 19th-century and 20th-century collections include the famous *Guernica* by Picasso, a number of important Spanish Surrealist and avant-garde works, including early works by Dalí, Miró paintings from the 1970s, and a fine collection of Cubist sculptures by Julio González. Major works by Antoni Tápies and by Spain's two greatest living sculptors, Jorge de Oteiza and Eduardo Chillida are also on show. The museum hosts regular retrospectives of both major artists and up-and-coming talent.

## Parque del Retiro (21)

Ⓜ Retiro, Príncipe de Vergara, Atocha, Ibiza 🕐 24 hours **Palacio de Velázquez** ☎ (91) 573 62 45 ● free ▮ ▯ ✦ ♬ ♿

The garden of the palace of the same name, built as a pleasure retreat for Philip IV (1621–55) ➠ 96. Retiro Park was opened to the public in 1869 by Isabel II, in exchange for a rent of 5 Ptas a year. In the center is a boating lake presided over by a monument to Alfonso XII which features an equestrian statue of the king by Mariano Benlliure and some magnificent examples of 19th-century Spanish sculpture. Exhibitions were held in the park buildings up until 1882. Today, the only two buildings still used for this purpose are Palacio de Velázquez and Palacio de Cristal. The latter is an iron-and-glass structure inspired by London's Crystal Palace and designed as a huge hothouse (currently undergoing renovation). Both palaces are decorated with *azulejos* (enamelled ceramic tiles) by Daniel Zuloaga.

## Not forgetting

■ **Estación de Atocha (22)** Plaza del Emperador Carlos V, 28012 *19th-century railway architecture, transformed by Rafael Moneo in 1992. The old wrought-iron structure was designed by Alberto del Palacio with the aid of Gustave Eiffel, and housed a winter garden. Opposite is the Ministry of Agriculture, a 19th-century building decorated with azulejos (ceramic tiles) and a large sculptural group.*
■ **Jardín Botánico (23)** Alfonso XII 8, 28014 ☎ (91) 420 30 17 🕐 daily 10am–6pm
*A remnant of Charles III's grand scheme for a scientific complex. Buildings and gateways by Francisco de Villalba. A peaceful botanical garden in which to examine a huge variety of plant species.*
■ **Observatorio Astronómico (24)** Alfonso XII 3 et 5, 28014 ☎ (91) 527 01 07 🕐 Mon.–Fri. 9am–2pm
*Part of the Botanic Garden. Built in 1790, and reconstructed in 1978.*
■ **Museo de Etnología (25)** Alfonso XII 68, 28014 ☎ (91) 530 64 18 🕐 Tue.–Sat. 10am–7.30pm, Sun. 10am–2pm
*The building dates from 1875. Exhibits from Africa, Asia and the Americas, including an interesting collection from the Philippines.*

■ Where to
eat ➙ 40
■ Where to
shop ➙ 144

21

21

23

22

Shown in New York until 1981, *Guernica* returned to Spain
after Franco's death in accordance with
Picasso's wishes.

20

20

## In the area
Some of the most animated scenes in Madrid are to be witnessed around Plaza de las Ventas on *corrida* (bullfight) days. Crowds of aficionados and devoted enthusiasts fill the streets after the fight.

▉ Where to stay ➡ 26

# What to see

### Plaza Monumental de las Ventas (26)
#### Alcalá 237, 28028 ☎ (91) 356 22 00

M *Ventas* ◯ **Corridas** *Mar.–Oct. : Sun. 7pm* **Feria de San Isidro** *May–June: daily 7pm* ● *400 Ptas–15,000 Ptas; Victoria 3, 28012 ☎ (91) 521 12 13 (tickets reserved in advance cost 20% more)*

This unusual building, erected in 1931, encloses one of the largest bullfighting arenas. Outside are monuments dedicated to two famous bullfighters, killed in the ring. The Feria of San Isidro (patron saint of Madrid) pits the most famous *toreros* and *novilleros* (novice bullfighters) against the most redoubtable fighting bulls or *novillos* (young bulls).

### Museo Taurino (27)
#### Alcalá 237, 28028 ☎ (91) 725 18 57

M *Ventas* ◯ *Tue.–Fri., Sun. 9.30am–2.30pm* ● *free*

This collection comprises costumes and bullfighting memorabilia from the 17th century to the present day. These include lithographs by Goya, a costume worn by the legendary Manolete on the day he was gored by a bull named Islero, the Papal Bull of Pius V (1567) banning corridas, and posters signed by Miquel Barceló and Eduardo Arroyo.

26

The traditional *corrida* involves six bulls and six *toreros*. It opens with a fanfare of trumpets and cymbals, after which the *alguacilillos*, or mounted constables, gallop in at the head of the *toreros* and their *cuadrillas* (teams of assistants). Each of the six fights is divided into three 'acts'. In the first *tercio* (third), the *torero* uses his pink cape to attract the bull while testing his temperament, condition and charge. The *suerte de varas* (pic-ing of the bull) is where the picador, mounted on a padded horse, applies his pic to the bull, causing it to bleed and thus to lose strength. In the second *tercio*, known as that of the *banderilleras* (short barbed sticks decorated with ribbons and colored paper), the *banderilleros* must test the bull and correct any defects in its line of charge. In the final *tercio*, called the *faena*, the *torero* faces the bull alone. Using his *muleta* (scarlet cape), he calls the bull, sidesteps it and forces it to turn around him by a series of skilful passes – performed increasingly slowly – and by retreating or standing still close to the bull's horns. When the matador's preliminary work is complete, he must kill the bull, going in over the horns to administer a clean, fatal blow.

## In the area

This huge landscape park in the English tradition was laid out in the early 1900s, and stretches from Plaza de España to the Ciudad Universitaria. It is fringed with museums and unusual monuments. The scene of repeated clashes during the Civil War, it is now overlooked by skyscrapers.

# What to see

## Museo de América (28)
### Reyes Católicos 6, 28040 ☎ (91) 543 94 37 ➡ (91) 577 67 42

🅜 Moncloa 🕙 Tue.–Sat. 10am–3pm; Sun., public holidays 10am–2.30pm ● 500 Ptas; students 200 Ptas; over-65s, children, Sun. free 🗂 🎦 🏛

The Museum of America documents the relationship between Spain and the American continent. Part of the collection comes from the *Real Gabinete de Historia Natural*, created in the 18th century. It is made up of objects brought back from scientific expeditions and from early excavations in Peru and the Mayan ruins of Palenque, and a selection of Mexican sacred objects, and subsequent acquisitions. The museum is organized into five sections: *Los Instrumentos del Conocimiento* examines myths and ideas about America from Columbus to the Enlightenment; *La Realidad de América* is devoted to the continent's geography and landscape, and its native peoples and populations; and *La Sociedad* looks at how the indigenous societies organized themselves. *La Religión* displays the Paracas Mummy and the Quimbayas Treasure, which is the most important pre-Hispanic collection of American gold objects. Finally, *La Comunicación* examines means of communication, and displays the jewel in the museum's crown – the Tro-Cortesian Codex, one of four Mayan manuscripts in existence, its hieroglyphs depicting scenes of daily life.

## Ermita de San Antonio de la Florida (29)
### Glorieta de San Antonio de la Florida 5, 28008 ☎ (91) 542 07 22

🅜 Príncipe Pío 🕙 Tue.–Fri. 10am–2pm, 4–8pm; Sat., Sun. 10am–2pm ● 300 Ptas; over-65s, students, children 150 Ptas; Wed., Sun. free 🗂 🎦

Designed by Italian architect Francesco Fontana, the hermitage contains Francisco de Goya's largest cycle of frescoes together with the artist's remains. The *Miracles of St Anthony*, which decorates the cupola, pendentives and transept, depicts Saint Anthony of Padua in Lisbon, where he brings a dead man back to life to testify to the innocence of his supposed assassin, the saint's father Don Martín de Bulloes. The hermitage also houses a small collection dedicated to the life of the artist. Next to it is a similar hermitage, built in 1928 for Catholic church services.

## Not forgetting

■ **Plaza de España (30)** *Two skyscrapers – a testament to Madrid's economic buoyancy during the early years of dictatorship. Edificio de España (1948–53) and the Torre de Madrid (1957) dominate the square. In the center of the plaza is a monument to Cervantes.*
■ **Templo de Debod (31)** Parque de la Montaña, 28008
*An Egyptian temple dating from the 4th century BC given to the city to thank its people for their contribution toward saving the temples of Nubia.*
■ **Museo Cerralbo (32)** Ventura Rodríguez 17, 28008 ☎ (91) 547 36 46
🕙 Tue.–Sat. 9.30am–2.30pm; Sun. 10am–2pm
*The residence and collection of Enrique de Aguilera y Gamboa, an aristocrat and respected archeologist. The museum provides an insight into the life of a late-19th-century nobleman.*

Where to eat ➡ 38
After dark ➡ 86

Cervantes looks down upon his two most famous creations: Don Quixote and Sancho Panza.

## In the area
Here, in one of the liveliest districts in Madrid, you can take in a museum or simply mingle with the crowds in Plaza Alonso Martínez.
■ Where to stay ➤ 22 ■ Where to eat ➤ 44 ■ After dark ➤ 68
➤ 78 ➤ 84 ■ Where to shop ➤ 130 ➤ 136 ➤ 138 ➤ 140

# What to see

## Biblioteca Nacional (33)
**Paseo de Recoletos 20, 28071 ☎ (91) 431 37 59 ➡ (91) 577 56 34**

Ⓜ *Colón, Serrano* Ⓝ *Mon.–Fri. 9am–9pm; Sat. 9am–2pm* ● *free, day pass for reading rooms available* ⊞ ▣

The building housing the National Library and Archaeological Museum (1866–92) was the most important structure built during the reign of Isabel II, and one of the first to use metal. The steps leading up to the library are decorated with 19th-century statues representing the fathers of the Castilian language. The pediment features an allegory of Arts and Letters with statues representing Study, Glory and Fame, and in the vestibule a statue by French sculptor Coullault Valeradu represents the polymath Don Marcelino Menéndez y Pelayo. The National Library has about 11 million volumes, one-third of which are housed in the main reading room. It also possesses a series of early printed books, manuscripts and prints, including engravings by Dürer.

## Museo Arqueológico Nacional (34)
**Serrano 13, 28001 ☎ (91) 577 79 12 ➡ (91) 431 68 40**

Ⓜ *Colón, Serrano* Ⓝ *Tue.–Sat. 9.30am–8.30pm; Sun. 9.30am–2.30pm*
● *500 Ptas, over-65s, students, children 250 Ptas, Sat. afternoon, Sun. morning free* ▣ ▣ ☎ *(91) 578 02 03* ▦

A vast collection of over 200,000 artifacts dating from prehistoric times to the 19th century. These include: a reproduction of the Altamira cave paintings, the gigantic bones of an elephant from Classical Antiquity, Iberian sculptures dating from the pre-Roman era, Roman mosaics from Las Estaciones, and the Treasure of Guarrázar – Visigothic votive crowns dating from the 7th century. Islamic culture is represented by lamps from the Alhambra in Grenada and by mosaics from the city of Medina Azahara in Córdoba. Finally, the Romanesque works of Maestro Mateo are among the jewels of the museum. Recent reorganization has transformed the museum into a first-rate institution with an educational slant.

## Not forgetting
■ **Museo Munícipal (35)** Fuencarral 78, 28004 ☎ (91) 588 86 72
Ⓝ Tue.–Fri. 9.30am–8pm; Sat., Sun. 9am–2pm
*The finest Baroque portal in Madrid. The former hospice, now a Municipal Museum, houses a scale model of 1830s Madrid, the work of chronicler Ramón de Mesonero Romanos and of Ramón Gómez de la Serna, Madrid's most devoted poet.*
■ **Museo Romántico (36)** San Mateo 13, 28004 ☎ (91) 448 10 71
Ⓝ Tue.–Sat. 10am–6pm; Sun. 10am–2pm
*Spanish Romanticism, in the form of paintings, objects and documents displayed in a neoclassical building dating from the 18th century.*
■ **Plaza de Colón (37)**
*A neo-Gothic statue of the legendary navigator and a rather unsuccessful sculptural group. The fountains represent Columbus' three ships.*

MUSEO MUNICIPAL DE MADRID

Fast becoming a major hub, this square is surrounded by various ministries and administrative centers. It is an amalgam of architectural styles, including some exceptionally fine 19th-century buildings.

# What to see

## Museo Nacional de Ciencías Naturales (38)
José Gutiérrez Abascal 2, 28006 ☎ (91) 561 86 00 ➠ (91) 564 50 78

Ⓜ *Nuevos Ministerios* 🕙 *Tue.–Fri. 10am–6pm; Sat. 10am–8pm; Sun. 10am–2.30pm* ● *Museum* 400 Ptas, over-65s, students, children 300 Ptas *Exhibition* 200 Ptas; over-65s, students, children 100 Ptas 🍴 🛈 ☎ (91) 564 61 69 🏢

Madrid's Natural Science Museum has been elevated to the rank of a world-class educational institution by the renovation of these palaces, built for the 1881 National Exhibition of Industry and the Arts. It houses a public library and a collection of over 3,500,000 artifacts. The permanent exhibits are organized around three principal themes: The History of the Earth and Life; To the Rhythm of Nature; and The Museum of the Museum. The insect collection is remarkable for its wide variety of species; the dinosaur section has a complete skeleton of a megathere dating back over two million years; and the vertebrates section includes such exhibits as the African Elephant and the Marsupial Wolf of Tasmania. Invertebrates are represented by a vast collection of molluscs from the Philippines and Cuba.

## Museo Lázaro Galdiano (39)
Serrano 122, 28006 ☎ (91) 561 60 84 ➠ (91) 561 77 93

Ⓜ *Rubén Darío* 🕙 *Tue.–Sun. 10am–2pm* ● *Ptas300; students Ptas150; over-65s, children, free on Sun.* 🍴

The private art collection of writer and editor José Lázaro Galdiano (1862–1947), is kept in the mansion he commissioned for his wealthy wife Doña Paula Florido. The collection includes *Head of The Saviour*, attributed to Leonardo da Vinci, and works by Goya and other European artists, especially British painters. The museum also houses a collection of French 14th-century ivory sculptures; Spanish, Italian, Byzantine and Limoges enamels; religious gold and silverwork, and jewelry; Renaissance medals and bronzes. Textiles and fans complete this unusual collection.

## Not forgetting

■ **Museo Sorolla (40)** Paseo General Martínez Blanco 37, 28010 ☎ (91) 310 15 84 🕙 *Tue.–Sat. 10am–3pm; Sun. 10am–2pm*
*The former home, with contents, of the painter Joaquín Sorolla y Bastida (1863–1923). A selection of works by the artist, generally considered to be Spain's best Impressionist painter. A delightful garden decorated with azulejos (ceramic tiles), fountains and pools.*
■ **Museo de Escultura al Aire Libre (41)**
Paseo de la Castellana 41, 28046
*A small open-air museum located under the flyover that links the calles of Juan Bravo and Eduardo Dato. A remarkable piece of civil engineering, the bridge was considered a model of urban design in the early 1970s. Displayed here are the works of 15 Spanish sculptors; notable among them are the Sirena Varada by Eduardo Chillida (comprising six tonnes of concrete suspended from the bridge), the mobile by Eusebio Sempere, Mère Ubu by Joan Miró, and Al otro lado del muro by José María Subirachs.*

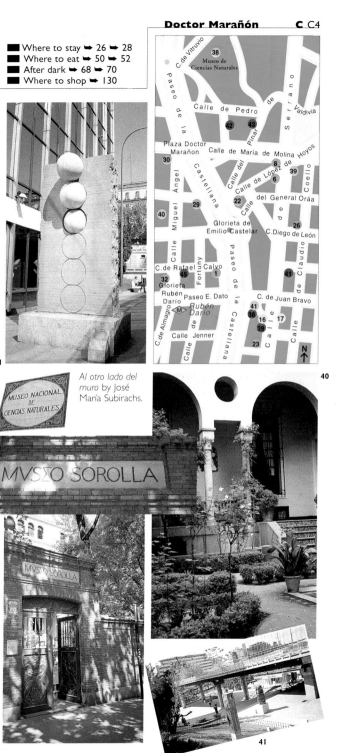

MUSEO NACIONAL DE CIENCIAS NATURALES

*Al otro lado del muro* by José María Subirachs.

MVSƎO SOROLLA

MVSƎO SOROLLA

The walk from Nuevos Ministerios to the Plaza de Castilla is like a journey through time, beginning with the architecture of the Franco dictatorship and finishing with the purest expressions of modernism. A curtain of stone, glass and metal stretches across these northern districts.

# What to see

## Azca (42)
### Paseo de la Castellana 79, 28046

Ⓜ️ *Nuevos Ministerios, Lima*

A commercial center covering some 500 acres ➡ 142, the Azca complex sprang up during the final years of the Franco dictatorship. The building that best typifies the avant-garde architecture of the 1970s is the skyscraper designed by Javier Sáenz de Oiza, its smooth bronze-glass walls serving as a symbol of economic might over the people (and a nod to Frank Lloyd Wright). The Torre Europa and Torre Picasso are equipped with a fiber-optic network controlling light, temperature and communication systems, and the Torre Picasso, designed by Minoru Yamasaki (architect of the World Trade Center in New York), is the tallest skyscraper in Madrid. The Windsor tower by Genaro Alas and Pedro Casariego (Raimundo Fernández Villaverde, 65) is distinguishable by its cylindrical, smooth-surfaced structure. The most eye-catching Azca building is the Sollube, which has a 'chain-mail' structure of aluminium and white lacquer and a green-glass exterior.

## Puerta de Europa (43)
### Plaza de Castilla, 28046

Ⓜ️ *Plaza de Castilla*

These two leaning towers rise to a height of over 370 feet, and tilt toward one another at an angle of 14.3°, forming a sort of *puerta* (door). Their green, smoked-glass surfaces reflect the surrounding buildings and the Madrid skyline. For architectural experts, the Puerta de Europa is the definitive skyscraper, arguably the most important architectural motif of the 20th century. The two towers seem to defy gravity, appearing locked in conflict. They are home to hundreds of offices.

## Nuevos Ministerios (44)
### Plaza de San Juan de la Cruz, 28003

Ⓜ️ *Lima*

The idea of bringing together the various government ministries within a single complex was the brainchild of the Spanish Republic. The project was completed under Franco at the end of the 1940s. This may explain the incongruous existence of a monument to the socialist Minister of Public Works, Indalecio Pieto, together with a monument to the dead dictator himself.

### Not forgetting

■ **Palacio de Congresos (45)** Paseo de la Castellana 99, 28046
☎ (91) 337 81 00 🕐 8am–8pm
*A conference center and entertainment venue. The frieze by Joan Miró was added to the façade in 1980.*

■ **Estadio Santiago Bernabéu (46)** Paseo de la Castellana 104, 28046 ☎ (91) 344 00 52
*Home of the Real Madrid football club. A model of 1940s 'sports architecture'.*

■ Where to stay ➥ 30 ➥ 32 ■
Where to eat ➥ 60 ➥ 64 ■ After dark
➥ 68 ➥ 72 ➥ 80 ➥ 82 ■ Where to
shop ➥ 142

44

Political figures of the
2nd Republic: I Pieto
and F Largo Caballero.

43

42

42

45

**Paradores de turismo**
State-owned buildings, usually former castles, palaces or
monasteries, converted into luxury hotels. Book in
advance. *Requena 3, 28013 Madrid* ☎ *(91) 516 66 66*
➡ *(91) 516 66 57 or (91) 516 66 58*

# Further afield

# 22
# Days out

## Sports and pastimes

### Airships
*Globos y dirigibles Boreal*
☎ (91) 561 39 68

### Cycling
*Federación Madrileña de Ciclismo*
☎ (91) 320 44 95

### Golf
*Federación de Golf*
☎ (91) 556 71 34

### Paragliding
*Hombre Pájaro*
☎ (91) 532 82 50

### Hiking
*Taller de naturaleza Las Acacias*
☎ (91) 465 45 99

### Bungee jumping
*Sport Adrenalin*
☎ (91) 365 19 23

### Horse-riding
Individual lessons, courses and rides.
*Posta de Corpes*
*Cañada de "El Arenal" - Cadalsos de los Vidrios (Par la C-501, carretera Plasencia)*
☎ (91) 861 14 16
● 2200 Ptas for 1 hour

### Skiing
Navacerrada and Valcotos are the two ski resorts closest to Madrid.
Information:
**ATUDEM**
*(Asociación Turística de Estaciones de Esquí y Montaña)*
☎ (91) 359 15 57

## Basic facts

San Lorenzo del Escorial, Aranjuez and Alcalá de Henares are part of the Comunidad de Madrid, one of Spain's 15 autonomous local authorities. Segovia and Toledo belong to Castilla y León and Castilla-La Mancha respectively.

# Further afield

## Segovia (13–17)

90 km north-west of Madrid

🚊 C-8b train, journey time 1 hr 49 min
● One-way ticket 750 Ptas
From Atocha or Chamartín Stations

🚌 La Sepulvedana Journey time 1 hr 30 min
● One-way ticket 765 Ptas
From Palos de la Frontera 16, 28045
☎ (91) 530 48 00
🚗 N VI and N 603
If you have time, leave the N VI at Collado Villalba and take the C 610 across the Sierra to Puerto de Navacerrada ➡ 111, a busy ski resort, and down to Valsaín and Granja de San Ildefonso.

**Tourist office**
Plaza Mayor 10, 40001
☎ (921) 46 03 34

## San Lorenzo del Escorial (5–8)

50 km north-west of Madrid

🚊 C-8a train Journey time 1 hr
● One-way ticket 365 Ptas
From Atocha or Chamartín Stations

🚌 Herranz Journey time 1 hr
● One-way ticket 380 Ptas
From La Moncloa
☎ (91) 890 41 00
🚗 N VI and M 505

**Tourist office**
Florida Blanca 10, 28200
☎ (91) 890 15 54

## Toledo (18–22)

70 km south of Madrid

🚊 C-3 train Journey time 1 hr 15 min
● One-way ticket 615 Ptas
From Atocha Station

🚌 Journey time 1 hr 30 min
● One-way ticket 570 Ptas
From Estación Sur, Méndez Álvaro, 28045
☎ (91) 468 42 00
🚗 N 401 Park by the city walls

**Tourist office**
Puerta Visagra, 45003
☎ (925) 22 08 43

Segovia 1317

San Lorenzo del Escorial 5, 8

## Alcalá de Henares
(1–4)

33 km north of Madrid

🚉 C-2 train
Journey time 35 min
● One-way ticket 305 Ptas
From Atocha or Chamartín Stations

🚌 Empresa bus
Journey time 30 min
● One-way ticket 250 Ptas
From Avenida de América 34, 28028 ☎ (91) 356 23 07

🚗 N II ( Barcelona)

**Tourist office**
Callejón de Santa María 1, 28801
☎ (91) 889 26 94

## Aranjuez
(9–12)

47 km south of Madrid

🚉 C-3 train
Journey time 45 min
● One-way ticket 465 Ptas
From Atocha Station

**El Tren de la Fresa**
Journey time approx 1 hr
● Roundtrip 2950 Ptas; children 1800 Ptas;
From Atocha Station Sat. and Sun. 10am (does not operate in August)
☎ (901) 22 88 22
A steam locomotive takes you along a line opened in 1851 to Aranjuez, the strawberry capital.

🚌 journey time 1 hr 15 min
● One-way ticket 340 Ptas
From Estación Sur, Méndez Álvaro, 28045
☎ (91) 468 42 00

🚗 N IV (toward Andalusia) You may be able to park on the esplanade beside the Palace

**Tourist office**
Plaza de San Antonio 9, 28300
☎ (91) 891 04 27

## In the area

Once an important Roman city, in the Middle Ages, Alcalá became an Arab market town rivaling that of Toledo ➡ 122. The old streets and 14th-century walls remain, as does the Castilian-style Plaza Mayor. The medieval and Renaissance nucleus has been declared a historic monument.

# Further afield

### Universidad Complutense (1)

Founded by Cardinal Cisneros in 1495, the Universidad Complutense (*Complutum* was the Roman name of the city) formed the cultural hub of the town. The university consisted of 'major' and 'minor' colleges, together with numerous convents and churches. Among the students were humanists, politicians and great theologians such as Quevedo, Francisco Suárez and Saint Ignatius Loyola. Miguel de Cervantes – the famous author of *Don Quixote* – was born here in 1547. In 1561 Philip II transferred the capital to Madrid, though the town kept its university status until 1836, when the Complutense was moved to Madrid, causing Alcalá to slide into decline.

### Colegio de San Ildefonso (2)
**Plaza de Santo Domingo, 28801 ☎ (91) 885 40 00**

🕐 *daily 10am–10pm* ● *free* 📷 ☎ *(91) 882 13 54 15* ● *300 Ptas* 🗐

Of the original building, only the Mudéjar amphitheater, with its fine coffered ceiling and plateresque rostrum, survives. The College façade is one of the purest examples of the plateresque style, so-called because its intricacy resembles worked silver (*platero* means silversmith). It was built in 1537 to a design by Rodrigo Gil de Hontañón, architect of the Cathedral of Segovia ➡ 120. Only two of the three great cloisters survive: the Baroque-style *Patio de Santo Tomás de Villanueva*, and the *Patio Trilingüe*, built in Italian Renaissance style.

### Iglesia Magistral (3)
**Plaza de los Santos Niños, 28801**

🕐 *Mass 9.15am, 12.15pm, 6pm, 8pm*

The Iglesia Magistral was erected at the beginning of the 16th century in a style inspired by the Cathedral of Toledo ➡ 122. It contains the tomb of the great Baroque sculptor Gregorio Fernández and an altarpiece by Felipe Vigarny, dating from the early 16th century.

### Convento de San Bernardo (4)
**Plaza de las Bernardas, 28801 ☎ (91) 888 11 22**

🕐 *Church* 📷 *daily* ☎ *(91) 882 13 54 15* ● *300 Ptas* 🗐

This convent, founded in 1618, was the work of Juan Gómez de Mora. Oval-shaped in plan, it contains six chapels, the principal one housing an altarpiece in the form of an architectural canopy. Adjoining the church are the Archbishop's Palace and the Madre de Dios convent, all part of the same complex.

## Not forgetting

■ **Teatro Cervantes** Cervantes, 28801 ☎ (91) 882 24 97 *One of the oldest classical theaters in Spain.* ■ **Convento de San Diego** Beatas 7, 28801 ☎ (91) 888 03 05 *The famous garrapiñadas (caramelized almonds) are prepared by the nuns.* ■ **La Hostería del Estudiante** Colegios 3, 28801 ☎ (91) 888 03 30 *Castilian cuisine. Famous migas con chocolate (fried bread dabbed with chocolate) – perfect with morning coffee.*

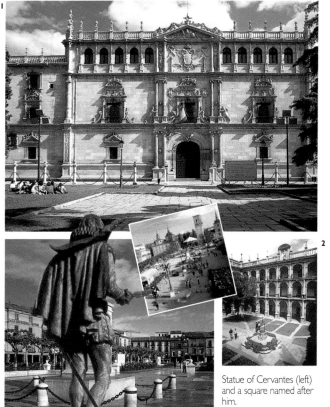

Statue of Cervantes (left) and a square named after him.

## In the area

The town here grew up around the monastery and palace complex commissioned by Philip II and completed in 1584. Set in the gardens of the park is the Casita del Príncipe, a tiny neoclassical palace designed by Juan de Villanueva, architect of the Prado Museum ➡ 96.

# Further afield

## Monasterio de San Lorenzo (5)
**Paseo Juan de Borbón, 28200 ☎ (91) 890 59 03**

◯ *Summer: Tue.–Sun. 10am–7pm; winter: Tue.–Sun. 10am–6pm* ● *950 Ptas; over-65s, students 350 Ptas, children free* 🔲 🔳 🎏 ▢ ⊞

King Philip II had this monastery built to commemorate the Spanish victory over the French at the Battle of San Quintín in 1557. It was to serve also as a pantheon for the king's father, Charles I of Spain, and for future Spanish monarchs. In 1563 Philip II commissioned a design from Juan Bautista de Toledo, who had worked in Rome with Michelangelo, and work continued under Juan de Herrera, with the involvement of the king himself. The result was dubbed 'the eighth wonder of the world'. The structure is impressive and austere, reflecting the personality of the king, who was the supreme defender of Counter-Reformation ideas. The building forms an immense rectangle. Its long façade runs 680 feet, with four patios and represents the martyrdom of St Laurence (he was roasted to death on a gridiron). A Flemish-style pinnacle tower rises from each of its four corners. A statue of San Lorenzo and the Hapsburg coat of arms are the only ornamentation on its main face.

### The library (6)

The library, clad in precious wood, is one of the highlights of the visit. The barrel-vaulted ceiling is decorated with allegorical figures representing the Seven Liberal Arts (Grammar, Rhetoric, Logic, Arithmetic, Music, Geometry and Astronomy). The bookshelves include fine reproductions of the first Castilian texts, a Mozarabic codex dating from the 10th century, the breviaries of the Catholic Monarchs and of Philip II, and numerous illuminated miniatures.

### Basílica (7)

The basilica's 295-foot high cupola contains the Capilla Mayor (Great Chapel), which features a remarkable Renaissance altarpiece. Note the sculptural groups, the work of Leone and Pompeo Leoni, on either side of the presbytery, one representing the Emperor and his family at prayer, the other Philip II and his family at prayer.

### Philip II's chambers (8)

These two simple rooms are surprisingly understated in comparison with the rest of the building. The bedroom has a balcony overlooking the Capilla Mayor, so that the king could hear Mass from his bed. The floor is covered with 16th-century Talavera tiles.

## Not forgetting

■ **Fonda Genara** Plaza de San Lorenzo 2, 28200 ☎ (91) 890 33 30
*Home cooking. Specialty: puchero (stew) de Luisa. Unusual décor.*
■ **La Comedia Nueva** Florida Blanca 20, 28200 ☎ (91) 890 44 11
*Café inside Charles III's Real Coliseo (a small 18th-century royal theater). Viennese-style late-19th-century decor.*

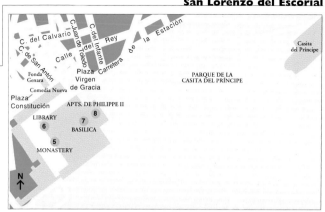

C. del Calvario
C. de san Antón
C. Juan de Toledo
C. del Infante
Calle del Rey
Carretera de la Estación

Fonda
Genara
Comedia Nueva

Plaza
Virgen
de Gracia

Plaza
Constitución

APTS. DE PHILIPPE II

LIBRARY

6

7

8

BASILICA

5

MONASTERY

PARQUE DE LA
CASITA DEL PRÍNCIPE

Casita
del Príncipe

N

**6**

**5**

**5**

## In the area

A fine example of a royal town, now a historic monument. At the end of the 15th century the Catholic Monarchs made it their *Real Sitio* (royal site). In the 16th century, Philip II built a new palace here. Philip V made this the Court's summer residence at the start of the 18th century.

 # Further afield

### The town (9)

The plans for the town were drawn up in 1747 by Ferdinand VI and Italian architect Bonavía. The streets were laid out in Baroque style, on a grid plan, with grand avenues converging on the palace. It was here that the Court witnessed some of the most momentous events in Spanish history, such as the *motín* (riot) of Aranjuez in 1808 – the conspiracy which paved the way for the Napoleonic invasion. The buildings are well preserved, and include a number of three- and four-storey houses dating from the 18th and 19th centuries with gardens and courtyards. The residences of the *oficios y caballeros* on Plaza de San Antonio, the palace of the Dukes of Medinaceli (now a restaurant), the hospital of San Carlos and the Convento de San Pascual are all worth seeing.

### Palacio real (10)
**Avenida del Palacio Real ☎ (91) 891 07 40**

🕐 *June–Sep.: Mon., Wed.–Sun. 10am–6.30pm; Oct.–May: Mon., Wed.–Sun. 10am–5.30pm* ● *500 Ptas; over-65s, students, children 250 Ptas, Wed. free* 🔲 🔲

The main body of the palace, in the fashionable Baroque style of the 18th century, was enlarged by the addition of two neoclassical wings, designed by Sabatini, which flank the Plaza Armería.

### Jardín de la Isla (11)
**Behind the palace**

🕐 *Tue.–Sun. 8am–8.30pm* ● *free*

A superb series of promenades modeled on Versailles. The paths and formal walks are punctuated by monumental fountains, arbors and magnificent trees, and cooled by the Tajo (Tagus) river.

### Jardín del Príncipe (12)
**Reina, en direction de la Casa del Labrador**

🕐 *Gardens Tue.–Sun. 8am–8.30pm* ● *free Casa del Labrador 10am–6.15pm* ● *425 Ptas, over-65s, students, children 225 Ptas* 🔲 *Casa de Marinos 10am–6.15pm* ● *325 Ptas, over-65s, students, children 225 Ptas*

A garden laid out for the young Charles IV (1788–1808). Planted with a rich variety of trees, the garden covers almost 400 acres and is the perfect setting for a stroll. The Empire-style Casa del Labrador was formerly a Bourbon hunting lodge, and is well worth visiting for its collection of clocks. The Casa de Marinos is now a boating museum where Court barges are displayed.

## Not forgetting

■ **Casa Pablo** Almíbar 42, 28300 ☎ (91) 891 14 51 *Specialties: pheasant, suckling pig, lamb, seafood.* ■ **La Rana Verde** Reina 1, 28300 ☎ (91) 891 32 38 *The dining rooms and terraces are worth a visit, but for the view over the Tajo rather than for the food.* ■ **El Bodegón** Gobernador 62, 28300 ☎ (91) 892 51 73 *Occupies the old brick wine cellars and stables of the Medinaceli palace. Suckling pig and lamb roasted over a wood fire.*

The Tajo river and fountains of
Aranjuez cool the arid plains of Castile.

## In the area

This historic town, now a world heritage site, is perched on a granite rock between the Eresma and Clamores rivers. Originally a Roman settlement, it became a major center of textile and livestock production during the Middle Ages.

 # Further afield

### The aqueduct (13)
#### Extra-muros, Plaza del Azoguejo

The aqueduct is Segovia's most famous monument, and the best preserved building of the Western Roman Empire. Bringing water from 8 miles away to the Plaza del Azoguejo, where it reaches a height of 92 feet, it dates from the 2nd century AD, and is made of granite blocks joined together without the aid of mortar.

### Plaza de San Martín (14)

🕐 *Keep* times vary **Church** Mass 11.30am, 12.30pm, 9pm

Site of the Romanesque church of San Martín. The Lozoya tower is a splendid example of a 14th-century fortified residence. A fine group is formed by the Renaissance-style Bornes Palace, the house known as the '15th-century house' and the Library.

### The Cathedral (15)
#### Plaza Mayor, 40006 ☎ (921) 46 22 05

🕐 *Museum and cloisters* daily 9.30am–7pm ● 250 Ptas 🗖

Begun in 1525, this is the last of the great Gothic cathedrals in Spain. Perched at the highest point of the town, the three naves above the altar rise to 108 feet. Between the cathedral and the Alcázar, look out for the Romanesque church of San Estéban with its elegant, tapering tower.

### El Alcázar (16)
#### Plaza de la Reina Victoria Eugenia, 40003 ☎ (921) 46 07 59

🕐 *spring–summer: daily 10am–7pm; autumn–winter: daily 10am–6pm* ● 375 Ptas, children 175 Ptas 🗖 🖥 🏛

In the 15th century Isabella the Catholic's father decided to erect a palace over a 12th-century tower. the Disney-style castle, all towers and turrets, now houses a military museum.

### Iglesia de la Vera Cruz (17)
#### Carretera Zamarramala ☎ (921) 43 14 75

🕐 *Apr.–Sep.: Tue.–Sat. 10.30am–1.30pm, 3.30–7pm; Oct.–Mar.: Tue.–Sun. 10.30am–1.30pm, 3.30–6pm* ● 175 Ptas 🗖 ⛰

Built on a dodecagonal (twelve-sided) plan, this beautiful church belonging to the Knights Templar is well worth a visit. Its bell tower offers a breathtaking view over the town and the Alcázar.

## Not forgetting

■ **Mesón Casa Cándido** Plaza del Azoguejo 5, 40001 ☎ (921) 42 51 03 *A renowned restaurant overlooking the aqueduct. Specialties include milk-fed lamb and pork.*
■ **Casa Duque** Cervantes 12, 40001 ☎ (921) 46 24 87 *Said by many to be the best restaurant in Segovia. Garlic soup, bean stew with pigs' trotters and ears.*

**13**

The 128 pillars and 163 arches of the Roman aqueduct carried water to Segovia up until 1988.

**16**

**14**

## In the area

In 554 Toledo was the political and religious capital of Spain, and later became the seat of important councils. It was also a Moorish town. For some five centuries the three great cultures of the Iberian Peninsula – Muslim, Christian and Jewish – merged here.

# Further afield

### The Old Town (18)

Renowned for its damascenes (intricate, water-like inlays on steel) ➡ 134, Toledo has preserved its maze of medieval streets. The medieval Alcázar and Great Mosque were incorporated into a castle and cathedral, but the 16th-century Puerta de Bisagra and 12th–14th century Puerta del Sol at the entrance to the town can still be seen, as can the San Martín and Alcántara bridges, and the Moorish baths.

### The Cathedral (19)
**Arco de Palacio 2, 45001 ☎ (925) 22 22 41**

◷ Oct 1–Apr. 30: Mon.–Sat. 10.30am–1pm, 3.30–6pm, Sun. 10.30am–1.30pm, 4–6pm; May 1–Sep. 30: Mon.–Sat. 10.30am–1pm, 3.30–7pm, Sun. 10.30am–1.30pm, 4–6pm ● 500 Ptas; students 400 Ptas ▤ ⊞

The cathedral was begun in 1227 and completed in 1493. Its interior reveals various styles – note the Flamboyant Gothic high altar and the Renaissance choir and stalls. Worth seeing are the *Transparente* (screen) by Narciso Tomé, and the museum, which features works by El Greco and Van Dyck.

### Santa María la Blanca (20)
**Reyes Católicos 2, 45002 ☎ (925) 22 72 57**

◷ Oct. 1–Apr. 30: daily 10am–1.45pm, 3.30–6.45pm; May 1–Sep. 30: daily 10am–1.45pm, 3.30–5.45pm ● 500 Ptas ▤ ⊞

This stunning five-aisled Almohad mosque dating from the 11th century was transformed into a synagogue at the end of the 12th century, and became a church in the 15th century. The original horseshoe arches and interlaced decoration have been retained.

### Iglesia de Santo Tomé (21)
**Plaza del Conde 1, 45002 ☎ (925) 25 60 98**

◷ daily 10am–1.45pm, 3.30–6.45pm ● 150 Ptas

A 14th-century church with a Mudéjar tower, and El Greco's *Burial of the Count of Orgaz* (1586), painted specifically for the church.

### Mezquita Cristo de la Luz (22)

🔑 If you can find the person with the keys…

A tiny mosque completed in 999, as testified by the Kufic inscription. The only entirely Moorish monument in the town, it was built in the Caliph style, with Visigothic columns and horseshoe arches.

## Not forgetting

■ **Parador Nacional de Turismo Conde de Orgaz** Paseo los Cigaralez, 45002 ☎ (925) 22 18 50 *Splendid views over the town. La Mancha cuisine.* ■ **Casa Aurelio** Sinagoga 6, 45001 ☎ (925) 22 20 97 *Castilian cuisine.* ■ **Asador Adolfo** Granada 5, 45001 ☎ (925) 22 73 21 *Traditional cooking meets nouvelle cuisine.*

# **Where to shop**

## **Where to shop**
Look for luxury goods in the Salamanca distinct; jewelry in Calle Serrano and Gran Vía; fashion in Calle Almirante; traditional Spanish styles around the Puerta del Sol; department stores on Calle Serrano.

## **Sales**
*Rebajas de temporada* – seasonal sales – are held twice a year: January–February and June–July.

## What to bring back

A torero's costume, a flamenco dress, castanets, a mantilla, a Spanish hairnet and a fan; a string of *Majorica* pearls and a piece of damascene work from Toledo; leather or a Real Madrid jersey; a fashionable handbag or shoes; olive oil, *jamón Serrano* and *turrón*.

# 60
# Shops
THE INSIDER'S FAVORITES

# Where to shop

### El Caballo Cojo (1)
**Segovia 7, 28012 ☎ (91) 366 43 90**

Ⓜ Sol, Ópera **Handicrafts, ceramics** 🕐 Mon.–Fri. 10am–2pm, 5–8.30pm; Sat. 10am–2pm; closed August ▭

Behind a 19th-century shop front is a magnificent array of ceramics reproduced in period styles. Particularly impressive are the blown glass objects from Mallorca in their characteristic blue, writing desks, candelabra and a collection of holy-water basins priced between 1000 Ptas and 40,000 Ptas.

### Monsy (2)
**Plaza Mayor 20, 28012 ☎ (91) 548 15 14**

Ⓜ Sol **Souvenirs** 🕐 Mon.–Sat. 9.30am–1.30pm, 4.30–8pm ▭

Lovers of kitsch will be spoilt for choice among this feast of bric-à-brac: bottles of Tío Pepe made in Jerez, bullfighters' costumes, castanets, El Cid's sword, Real Madrid merchandise ➡ 108, and damascene objects from Toledo ➡ 122.

### Justo Algaba (3)
**Paz 4, 28012 ☎ (91) 523 35 95 ➡ (91) 523 37 17**

Ⓜ Sol **Bullfighters' costumes, flamenco-style dresses** 🕐 Mon.–Fri. 10am–2pm, 5–8pm; Sat. 10am–2pm ▭

This tailor serves some of the biggest names in bullfighting ➡ 100. Behind the window protected from the sun's rays, you can buy stockings, a *montera* (bullfighter's hat) and pumps to transform yourself into the perfect *torero*. From the workshop you can order an authentic made-to-measure *traje campero* (the suit worn by bullfighters for out-of-town practise sessions) or a flamenco-style dress with all the proper accessories. Prices depend on the number of hours of work involved and the quality of the materials and embroidery.

### Seseña (4)
**Cruz 23, 28012 ☎ (91) 531 68 40**

Ⓜ Sol **Capes** 🕐 Mon.–Fri. 10am–3pm, 4.30–8pm; Sat. 10am–2pm ▭

Picasso, Hemingway and Hillary Clinton are among the many who have been unable to resist Seseña's warm, dramatic Madrid-style capes. Seseña is now the only store specializing in this romantic garment. It is worth a visit just to admire the window display. Men's capes from 60,000 Ptas.

## Not forgetting
■ **Casa Yustas (5)** Plaza Mayor 30, 28012 ☎ (91) 366 58 34
*Every kind of headgear from military caps to the famous Andalusian headdresses.*
■ **El Riojano (6)** Mayor 10, 28012 ☎ (91) 366 44 82
*Living up to its reputation since 1855. Worth a visit as much for the décor as for the cakes.*

■ Where
to shop
➡ 144

2

4

# Where to shop

### Casa Jiménez (7)
**Preciados 42, 28013 ☎ (91) 548 05 26**

Ⓜ *Callao, Santo Domingo* **Shawls, mantillas** 🕐 *Mon.–Sat. 10.30am–1.30pm, 5.30–8pm* ▭

Manila shawls imported from the Philippines and mantillas of silken lace are the specialties of this store which claims to be 'the best-stocked and oldest in Spain'. For almost a century it has been selling sumptuous, hand-embroidered shawls in brilliant colors with oriental motifs. Originally worn to keep out the cold, in the 18th century they came to be regarded as fashion accessories. Now part of Spanish tradition, shawls are still very popular and are worn for special occasions. Machine-made shawls start at 5000 Ptas, top-of-the-range 40,000 Ptas.

### Casa Mira (8)
**Carrera de San Jerónimo 30, 28014**
**☎ (91) 429 67 96 ➡ (91) 429 82 21**

Ⓜ *Sol, Sevilla* **Turrón** 🕐 *Mon.–Sat. 9.30am–2pm, 6.30–9pm, Sun. 10.30am–2.30pm, 5.30–9pm* ▭

Turrón (Spanish nougat) and *mazapán* (marzipan) are top of every Spaniard's list of Christmas goodies. If you happen to be passing by during the festive season, don't be surprised to find an endless queue of *Madrileños* waiting their turn to buy the *turrón* and other treats made here since 1885. Try *turrones* from Segovia ➡ 120 or Alicante, flavored with nuts, coconut, fruit or chocolate, or guirlache, another type of nougat. About 4000 Ptas a kilo.

### Casa de Diego (9)
**Plaza Puerta del Sol 12, 28013 Madrid ☎ (91) 522 66 43**

Ⓜ *Sol* **Umbrellas, fans** 🕐 *Mon.–Sat. 9.45am–1.30pm, 4.30–8pm*
⬕ *Mesonero Romanos 4, 28013 ☎ (91) 521 02 23*

'Tomorrow it will rain' is the motto of this old store in the Puerta del Sol ➡ 94. Since 1858 they have been selling umbrellas made in their own workshops, as well as walking sticks, sunshades, shawls, mantillas, combs and a huge range of fans, made from paper, mother-of-pearl or gold. Fans start at 350 Ptas, but expect to pay 50,000 Ptas for hand-painted ones with mother-of-pearl blades.

## Not forgetting
■ **M. Gil (10)** Carrera de San Jerónimo 2, 28014 ☎ (91) 521 25 49
*Established 1880: mantillas, embroidered table linen from Lagartera (Toledo region ➡ 122), traditional hairnets, embroidered shawls and typical Madrileño costumes.*
■ **Carpincho (11)** Preciados 33, 28013 ☎ (91) 521 13 60
*Range of high-quality ceramics from Seville, appointed agent for Majorica pearls and Lladró porcelain.*
■ **Manuel Herrero (12)** Preciados 7–16, 28013 ☎ (91) 521 29 90
*Reasonably-priced leather fashions and shoes.*
■ **La Violeta (13)** Plaza de Canalejas 6, 28014 ☎ (91) 522 55 22
*This store has been selling its famous sweets, colored, flavored and shaped like violets, since 1915.*

Gran Vía
Callao M Plaza
del Callao
Calle Mesonero
C. Abada
Plaza del Carmen
Calle Aduana
10
5
M Sevilla
C. Cedaceros
C. de Jacometrezo
7
Calle
11
C. Veneras
C. Trujillos
Plaza San Martín
C.Misericordia
6
Calle del Carmen
Calle de Preciados
Maestro Victoria
Plaza del Carmen
Calle de la Montera
Calle de Alcalá
Calle de Sevilla
C. de Arlabán
Plaza Canalejas
Jerónimo
8
V. de la Vega
9
Calle Carrera San
13
Calle de Echegaray
C. Priora Flora
11
12
14
Calle del Arenal
Calle
11
Puerta del Sol
M Sol
C.C. Carrera San
C. Espoz y Mina
C. Victoria
Calle de la Cruz
Calle del Príncipe
23
22
N

13

8

8

13

9

7

11

10

## Basic facts

Madrid's shopping scene is dominated by El Corte Inglés where you will find everything from fashions to food all under one roof. More appealing are the smaller shopping malls incorporating small boutiques set in bright, stylish surroundings with plenty of bars and cafés; just the thing

# ◤ Where to shop

## El Corte Inglés (14)

Preciados 1-2-3-4, 28013 ☎ (91) 379 80 00 ➡ (91) 521 56 57

🅼 Sol *Fashions, records, tapes and CDs, books, toys* 🕐 *Mon.–Sat. 10am–9.30pm* 🍴 🔲 ♿ *Raimundo Fernández Villaverde 79, 28003* ☎ *(91) 556 33 00; Princesa 42, 28008* ☎ *(91) 542 48 00; Goya 76, 28009* ☎ *(91) 577 71 71; Goya 87, 28001* ☎ *(91) 577 71 71; Serrano 47, 28001* ☎ *(91) 432 93 00*

At the turn of the century, El Corte Inglés was just a tailor's workshop on Calle Preciados, specializing in gentlemen's outfits with a distinctly 'English' cut. As the years went by, their range of products and services increased enormously and Corte Inglés stores multiplied. Now the chain offers such services as coffee shops and restaurants, beauty and hairdressing salons, tobacconists, travel agencies and supermarkets. At present, Madrid has no fewer than sixteen shopping malls and stores under the banner of El Corte Inglés, all strategically situated and offering complementary services: the branch at Goya 76 sells fashions, leather goods, jewelry, perfumes and sportswear; along the street at Goya 87, the range includes household goods, books, photographic

14

for those who prefer relaxed, leisurely shopping.

equipment, CDs and videos. The huge selection of goods and brands, and the efficiency and quality of its services ensure the continued success of El Corte Inglés. It is now the only store in Madrid that can truly be called a 'department store'.

## Not forgetting

■ **El Jardín de Serrano**
**(15)** Goya 6–8, 28001
☎ (91) 577 00 12
*Winner of the European Design Prize in the shopping mall category. Elegant and well situated, with boutiques on two levels, a large café and a shady garden.*

■ **ABC Serrano (16)** Serrano 61, 28004 ☎ (91) 577 50 31
*Recently opened conversion of the old ABC and Blanco y Negro newspaper offices. Four levels of stores in a bright, congenial setting. Wonderful neo-plateresque façade on the Paseo de la Castellana side.*

■ **Multicentro Serrano 88 (17)** Serrano 88, 28006 ☎ (91) 547 50 01
*One of Madrid's very first shopping malls, containing fashion boutiques and gift stores, and a pleasant café.*

## In the area

Elegant stores and cafés, theaters and state-of-the-art movie theaters, the Gran Vía is a must for visitors. ■ Where to stay ➡ 18 ➡ 20 ■ After dark ➡ 72 ➡ 74 ■ What to see ➡ 94

# ➡ Where to shop

### Zara (18)
**Gran Vía 32, 28013 ☎ (91) 522 97 27 ➡ (91) 532 95 31**

Ⓜ Callao **Men's and women's ready-to-wear fashions** 🕐 Mon.–Sat. 10am–8.30pm ▬ 🚻 Princesa 63, 28008 ☎ (91) 543 24 15; Murillo 104, 28039 ☎ (91) 533 10 50

Ever since it opened, Zara has been a fashion phenomenon with dozens of branches all over Spain and in big cities around the world (including New York). The secret of their success is simple: up-to-date styles at unbeatable prices. All over Madrid, their shop windows display the latest trends in men's, women's and children's clothes, as well as shoes, handbags and other accessories.

### Casa del Libro (19)
**Gran Vía 29, 28013 ☎ (91) 521 21 13 ➡ (91) 522 77 58**

Ⓜ Gran Vía, Callao **Books** 🕐 Mon.–Sat. 10am–8.30pm ▬ 🚻 Maestro Victoria 3, 28013 ☎ (91) 521 48 98

Books on every imaginable subject take up the five levels of this huge store. With a permanent stock of around 500,000 volumes, it is one of Europe's biggest bookstores. Despite its size it is still a friendly place and it is easy to while away a pleasant afternoon browsing through its shelves. Casa del Libro recently opened a large foreign language section.

### Cortefiel (20)
**Gran Vía 27-76, 28013 ☎ (91) 522 00 93 ➡ (91) 522 19 99**

Ⓜ Gran Vía, Callao **Ready-to-wear fashions** ▬ 🕐 Mon.–Sat. 10am–8.30pm 🚻 Aguileras 62, 28015 ☎ (91) 543 04 05; Paseo de la Castellana 146, 28046 ☎ (91) 458 29 30

With various branches scattered around the city, this chain store has, since the 1980s, sold reasonably-priced casual fashions in fairly classic styles. A little further along the Gran Vía (at no. 59), Springfield caters for younger, sports-minded customers.

### Grassy (21)
**Gran Vía 1, 28013 ☎ (91) 532 10 07 ➡ (91) 575 48 67**

Ⓜ Banco de España, Gran Vía **Jewelry** 🕐 Mon.–Fri. 9.45am–3.30pm, 4.30–8pm, Sat. 9.45am–3.30pm ▬ 🚻 José Ortega y Gasset 17, 28006 ☎ (91) 577 94 35

One of Madrid's oldest and most prestigious jewelry stores, with the style and atmosphere of a bygone age.

## Not forgetting

■ **Aldao (22)** Gran Vía 15, 28013 ☎ (91) 522 11 56 *A classic among Madrid jewellers.*
■ **Madrid Rock (23)** Gran Vía 25, 28013 ☎ (91) 523 26 52 *Music store catering for every taste, with the accompaniment of very loud Spanish rock.*

**21**

**133**

## In the area

In the neighborhood west of the Gran Vía, traditional jewellers and ceramics stores stand side-by-side with modern fashion boutiques. All of them contribute to the buzz of this cosmopolitan thoroughfare.
■ Where to stay ➡ 20 ■ Where to eat ➡ 38 ■ After dark ➡ 80

# Where to shop

### Antigua Casa Talavera (24)
**Isabel la Católica 2, 28013 ☎ (91) 547 34 17**

M *Santo Domingo* **Ceramics** ◯ *Mon.–Fri. 10am–1.30pm, 5–8pm; Sat. 10am–1.30pm*

This turn-of-the-century store is an Aladdin's cave of traditional Spanish pottery, with reproductions of pieces dating from the 10th to the 18th century. These are manufactured in family-run workshops in Talavera (a little village in the Toledo region ➡ 122), Sevilla, Puente del Arzobispo, Granada and Manises. Baptismal fonts, candelabra, tiles (on which they will engrave a proverb of your choice), decorative plates and tureens are all sold here.

### Hernández (25)
**Gran Vía 56, 28013 ☎ (91) 547 06 54**

M *Callao* **Handicrafts, jewelry, fans** ◯ *Mon.–Sat. 10am–1.30pm, 4.30–8pm* ▭

The window of this traditional store looks like any other in the neighborhood, but go in and you will discover a wonderful array of feminine finery: fans, *Majorica* pearls, costume jewelry and damascene (steel with inlaid gold) knick-knacks from Toledo ➡ 122.

### Zaraúz (26)
**Gran Vía 45, 28013 ☎ (91) 547 17 36**

M *Callao* **Men's and women's ready-to-wear fashions** ◯ *Mon.–Sat. 10am–2pm, 3–8.30pm* ▭ ◫ *Goya 7–9, 28001 ☎ (91) 435 49 48*

Locals love Zaraúz for the fine quality and discreet, elegant style of its suits and sportswear. Remarkable selection of neckties, prices up to 12,000 Ptas.

### Regalos Ar (27)
**Gran Vía 46, 28013 ☎ (91) 522 68 69 ➡ (91) 531 56 47**

M *Callao* **Handicrafts, porcelain, jewelry** ◯ *Mon.–Sat. 10am–8pm* ▭

A modern store whose window displays an endless variety of gifts and attractive souvenirs, all 'made in Spain'. These include stunning porcelain, including a famous collection of figurines by Lladró for whom Regalos Ar is an appointed agent. Equally outstanding are the *Majorica* pearls, glassware and craft items.

## Not forgetting

■ **Camper (28)** Gran Vía 54, 28013 ☎ (91) 547 52 23
*An internationally-famous Spanish firm whose first priority is comfort. Offers a huge range of designer shoes and boots, from the classic to the trendy, with some very witty touches.*
■ **Bravo Java (29)** Gran Vía 54, 28013 ☎ (91) 522 22 00
*Renowned for the range and quality of its shoes.*

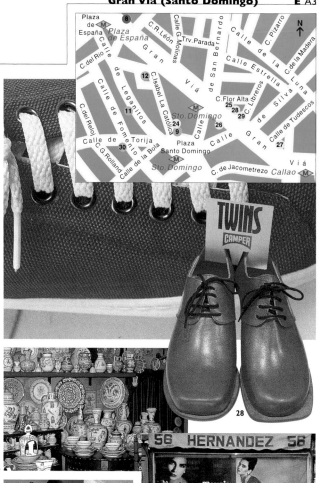

*Majorica* pearls, made on the island of Mallorca, are the nearest thing to real and cultured pearls. It's very hard to tell the difference.

## In the area

Calle Almirante was the place to be in the heady days of 1980s fashion. It turned out to be a flash in the pan, but some talent still survives.

■ Where to stay ➡ 22 ■ Where to eat ➡ 44 ■ After dark ➡ 68 ➡ 76 ➡ 78 ➡ 84 ■ What to see ➡ 104

# Where to shop

### Ararat (30)
#### Almirante 10-11, 28004 ☎ (91) 531 81 56 ➡ (91) 532 10 47

Ⓜ *Colón, Banco de España* **Ready-to-wear women's fashions** 🕒 *Mon.–Sat. 11pm–2pm, 5–8.30pm* ▭

Although the neighborhood's golden age is over, Ararat continues to be on the pulse with its designer boutiques, including Vertigo, VMR, Rosas Rojas and A Menos Cuarto. Evening and town wear.

### Piamonte (31)
#### Piamonte 16, 28004 ☎ (91) 522 45 80

Ⓜ *Colón, Banco de España* **Accessories, jewelry** 🕒 *Mon.–Sat. 10.30am–2pm, 5–8.30pm* ▭ ⬧ *Marqués del Monasterio 5, 28004 ☎ (91) 576 7350*

Since the 1980s, this store has gained a strong reputation and a large clientele. Inside, accessories for every occasion are displayed in simple, attractive surroundings: belts, purses, gloves and a small but interesting collection of reasonably-priced jewelry. From Piamonte's own workshops you can order top-quality bags in leather, canvas or other materials, in the color of your choice. Orders take ten days. Around 15,000 Ptas.

### Joaquín Berao (32)
#### Conde de Xiquena 13, 28004 ☎ (91) 310 16 20

Ⓜ *Colón, Banco de España* **Jewelry** 🕒 *Mon.–Sat. 10.30am–2pm, 5–8.30pm* ▭ ⬧ *Conde Aranda 7, 28001 ☎ (91) 576 7350*

In the mid-Eighties, Joaquín Berao left his experimental studio and set up this little jewelry store to sell his own creations. Since then, he has extended his collections of men's and women's jewelry and his fame has spread beyond the borders of Spain. His most renowned creation is the *raspa* (fishbone) a flexible necklet shaped like a fishbone. Specializing in silver jewelry, Joaquín Berao also makes pieces in painted or gilded bronze. The cheapest items are affordable: necklaces between 9000 Ptas and 80,000 Ptas.

## Not forgetting

■ **Patrimonio Comunal Olivarero (33)** Mejía Lequerica 1, 28004 ☎ (91) 308 0505 *All the olive oils sold here are from renowned producers.*
■ **Vime (34)** Augusto Figueroa 18, 28004 ☎ (91) 532 0240
*There are more than a dozen shoe stores concentrated in Calle Augusto Figueroa and the surrounding streets. Ends of lines or models used for fashion exhibitions are offered at bargain prices. This is one of Madrid's oldest stores, selling men's and women's shoes.*
■ **Excrupulus Net (35)** Almirante 7, 28004 ☎ (91) 521 72 44
*Small boutique with a fine selection of the latest in shoes. Around 18,000 Ptas a pair.*
■ **Almirante 23 (36)** Almirante 23, 28004 ☎ (91) 308 12 02
*For the collector: postcards, cameras, tin boxes, bottles, spectacles, pictures, puzzles, lead soldiers and many more curiosities.*

# Calle Almirante    E A4

**31**

**31**

Joaquín Berao's
creations are
known worldwide
and are famous for
their sculptured
shapes.

**35**

Aceite de Oliva
Virgen Extra
Vitoliva

**33**

**36**

**32**

## In the area

Some of Madrid's most stylish boutiques are in the neighborhood east of Paseo de Recoletos, behind the Biblioteca Nacional. ■ Where to stay ➡ 22 ■ Where to eat ➡ 42 ➡ 44 ➡ 46 ■ After dark ➡ 78 ➡ 84 ■ What to see ➡ 96 ➡ 104 ■ Where to shop ➡ 130 ➡ 144

# ➡ Where to shop

### Ispahan (37)
**Serrano 5, 28001** ☎ (91) 575 20 12 ➡ (91) 577 76 41

Ⓜ *Retiro* **Carpets** Ⓥ *Mon.–Sat. 10am–2pm, 4.30–8.30pm* ▣

This carpet store is worth a detour both for its stock and for the building, which underwent major renovations in order to provide space for an antiques center, designers and galleries. Ispahan has now taken over the entire space to display tapestries and Persian, Turkish, Chinese, Tibetan and Caucasian carpets, as well as reproductions of 15th- and 16th-century Spanish cartoons.

### Farrutx (38)
**Serrano 7, 28001** ☎ (91) 576 94 93 ➡ (91) 576 34 08

Ⓜ *Serrano, Retiro* **Shoes, handbags** Ⓥ *Mon.–Sat. 10am–2pm and 5–8pm* ▣

This highly prestigious Spanish shoe manufacturer, famed for its original, elegant style, is a leader in its field for quality and design.

### Adolfo Domínguez (39)
**Serrano 18-36, 28001** ☎ (91) 576 70 53 ➡ (91) 435 86 92

Ⓜ *Serrano* **Ready-to-wear fashions for men and women** Ⓥ *Mon.–Sat. 10am–2pm, 5–8pm* ▣

Simple lines, comfort and sophistication, harmonious colors and natural fabrics characterize the clothes created by this designer who became famous in the 1980s for his motto 'pleats are beautiful'. Adolfo Domínguez has since gained international renown and his beautiful sinuous creations appear in boutiques around the world.

### Lœwe (40)
**Serrano 26, 28001** ☎ (91) 577 60 56

Ⓜ *Serrano* **Accessories, ready-to-wear fashions** Ⓥ *Mon.–Fri. 9.30am–2pm, 4–8.30pm* ▣ ⚑ *Palacio Miraflores, Carrera de San Gerónimo 15, 28014* ☎ (91) 360 61 00

Loewe specializes in leather, carefully selecting and treating the raw material to produce genuine works of art. As well as leather clothes, there are interesting silk scarves and neckties. Everything here is 'deluxe' – including the prices.

## Not forgetting

■ **La Pajarita (41)** Villanueva 14, 28001 ☎ (91) 435 74 54 *Madrid's other famous traditional candy store* ➡ *128. Candy in sixteen different flavors.*
■ **Roberto Verino (42)** Claudio Coello 27, 28001 ☎ (91) 577 60 56 *Talented designer of women's ready-to-wear fashions who emerged in the 1980s.*
■ **El Callejón de Jorge Juan (43)** Jorge Juan 14, 28001 *Little cul-de-sac with charming boutiques, away from the hustle and bustle of the city. In 1994, the city fathers awarded the tiny street a special prize for its contribution to the environment.*

Plaza de Colón

37

28

Jardines del Descubrimiento

Paseo de Recoletos

33

34

40

28  26

41

Calle de Recoletos

38

37

C. Salustiano Olozaga

19

16

Plaza de la Independencia

22

16

M Serrano

Calle

de

Goya

15

Serrano

Coello

Lagasca

60

42

40

Calle

de

Jorge

Juan

43

39

Claudio

C.Puigcerda

29

de

de

Villanueva

C. del Conde de Aranda

Calle

Columela

Calle

Retiro

M

de

Alcalá

PARQUE DEL RETIRO

C. del Cid

Calle

Calle

N ↑

40

150 ANIVERSARIO  150 ANIVERSARIO  150 ANIVERSARIO

LOEWE
Madrid 1846

150 ANIVERSARIO

40

40

42

ROBERTO VERINO

40

42

38

139

# Where to shop

## Artespaña (44)
**Hermosilla 14, 28001 ☎ (91) 435 02 21 ➡ (91) 575 34 55**

Ⓜ Serrano **Handicrafts** ◐ *Mon.–Sat. 10.15am–2pm, 5–8.30pm* ▭

In this magnificent store, the national handicrafts organization offers a selection of furniture, accessories, fabrics and decorative items from Spain's finest craftspeople. Vases, tapestries and household linen are among the things that you can admire or buy here.

## Del Pino (45)
**Serrano 48, 28001 ☎ (91) 435 26 70 ➡ (91) 431 86 42**

Ⓜ Serrano **Jewelry** ◐ *Mon.–Sat. 10am–2pm, 5–8.30pm* ▭

A vast but well-chosen range of jewelry, in the latest shapes, colors and materials. The treasures displayed on the shelves and in the windows are hard to resist.

## Elena Benarroch (46)
**José Ortega y Gasset 14, 28006 ☎ (91) 435 51 44 ➡ (91) 431 49 60**

Ⓜ Núñez de Balboa **Furs** ◐ *Mon.–Sat. 10am–2pm, 4.30–8.30pm* ▭ �
Zurbaran 16, 28010 ☎ (91) 308 28 16

After devoting 17 years to revolutionizing fur design, Elena Benarroch turned her attentions to her firm's vast shop window, which she intended to be 'a place where people stop rather than simply pass by'. She achieved her objective. A spectacular Murano glass chandelier illuminates a space dedicated to sophisticated design. Luxury items carrying the best international labels are tastefully displayed. The range extends from mink coats to sable rugs, through handmade Santa María Novella soaps, cashmere coats from Loro Plana, Philip Treacy hats, and shoes and bags from Bottega Veneta. Our advice: take time to soak up the atmosphere.

## El Caballo (47)
**Lagasca 55, 28001 ☎ (91) 576 40 37 ➡ (91) 578 08 80**

Ⓜ Serrano **Saddlery and riding habits** ◐ *Mon.–Fri. 10am–2pm, 5–8.30pm; Sat. 10.15am–2pm, 5–6pm* ▭

Bags, suitcases, belts, boots, walking shoes, saddles, riding accessories – the store offers an endless selection of leather goods of the highest quality, and a huge array of articles and clothes whose shape and motifs are inspired by Andalusian style. Everything on sale is manufactured in Seville, where the first El Caballo workshop was founded in 1892.

### Not forgetting
■ **Santa (48)** Serrano 56, 28001 ☎ (91) 576 86 46
*Luxurious Madrid chocolate manufacturer. A feast for the eyes as well as the taste buds.*
■ **Oh ! Qué Luna (49)** Ayala 32, 28001 ☎ (91) 431 37 25
*Nightwear for all the family. A lovely, original selection of lingerie.*

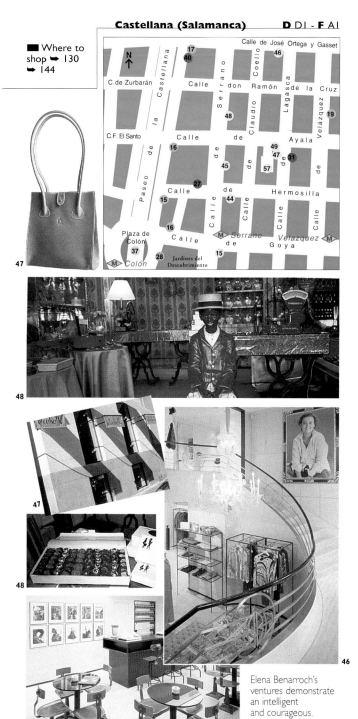

■ Where to shop ➥ 130
➥ 144

Elena Benarroch's ventures demonstrate an intelligent and courageous, creative talent.

## In the area

This is the most modern part of Madrid, where you will find lots of lively, practical shopping complexes. ■ Where to stay ➡ 30 ➡ 32 ■ Where to eat ➡ 58 ■ After dark ➡ 68 ➡ 72 ➡ 74 ■ What to see ➡ 108

# Where to shop

### Musgo (50)
**Paseo de la Habana 34, 28036** ☎ (91) 562 86 24 ➡ (91) 562 86 24

Ⓜ *Lima* **Gifts** Ⓧ *Mon.–Sat. 10am–noon, 1–9pm* ▣ Ⓧ *Hermosilla 34, 28001* ☎ *(91) 431 55 10 ; Serrano 18, 28001* ☎ *(91) 575 33 50*

What used to be a little gift store has become, 20 years later, a mighty chain with outlets all around the city. The shop windows are stunning at Christmas, when Musgo uses every trick in the book to attract customers. This store specializes in clothes, leather accessories, costume jewelry, watches, ornaments and practical household goods, including small items of furniture. There is also a recently-opened department selling children's and babies' clothes.

### Massimo Dutti (51)
**Paseo de la Habana 40, 28036** ☎ (91) 563 93 22

Ⓜ *Lima* **Men's and women's ready-to-wear fashions** Ⓧ *Mon.–Sat. 10am– 2pm, 5–8.30pm* ▣ Ⓧ *Velazquez 46, 28001* ☎ *(91) 431 77 90*

In the early 1980s a young entrepreneur revolutionized menswear stores by offering vast numbers of shirts in different styles but at the same price. It was a complete success and the numerous stores in the chain now offer even greater variety while sticking to the same principle. Today, Massimo Dutti dresses men from head to toe in quality garments at reasonable prices. Women, too, can now buy practical, comfortable clothes here for every occasion.

### Coronel Tapioca (52)
**Paseo de la Habana 52, 28036** ☎ (91) 562 64 68 ➡ (91) 563 37 40

Ⓜ *Lima, Concha Espina* **Fashions, sportswear and outdoor gear** Ⓧ *Mon.–Sat. 10am–2pm, 5–8.30pm* ▣ Ⓧ *Serrano 81, 28006* ☎ *(91) 563 22 21; Genova 23, 28004* ☎ *(91) 308 29 08; Hermosilla 31, 28001* ☎ *(91) 576 22 88*

Clothing and accessories for intrepid adventurers and urban explorers; all-purpose boots, flasks, mountaineers' hats, rucksacks, compasses, leather and linen bomber jackets, pocket flashlights and sweaters. Coronel Tapioca also stocks comfortable and inexpensive casual styles to wear around town.

### Not forgetting

■ **Moda Shopping (53)** Avenida General Perón 40, 28020 ☎ (91) 581 15 25 *Large shopping mall with more than 70 stores under one glass roof.*

■ **La Esquina del Bernabéu (54)** Avenida Concha Espina 1, 28036 ☎ (91) 344 06 43 *Shopping mall. On the top floor is a store devoted entirely to the Real Madrid football squad* ➡ *108.*

■ **Alexandra Bellinger (55)** Emilio Campión 19, 28002 ☎ (91) 561 76 38 *Internationally-renowned jewelry designer. Collections inspired by different periods and cultures. Unusual combinations of gold and stones.*

52

55

53

54

MODA
CENTRO COMERCIAL

TU GUIA

55

## Basic facts

Set aside at least a morning to mingle with the market crowds. Here, you will capture the authentic, or *castizo* atmosphere of the city. The Rastro, most famous of the flea markets, occupies what used to be the *barrios bajos* (working-class neighborhood). The markets specializing in

# ➡ Where to shop

## El Rastro (56)
### Ribera de Curtidores and surroundings, 28005

Ⓜ *Tirso de Molina, La Latina* **Flea market** 🕐 *Sun. and public holidays from 9am*

In the 16th century, makeshift stalls crowded this neighborhood's tanneries and abattoirs. The abattoirs have now gone, but the Rastro has become a Sunday institution. The market is a fascinating insight into Madrid life for the curious visitor and has become something of a ritual for the locals. Stop and take a look at some of the objects on offer. The stalls and stores with their idiosyncratic displays are irresistible: bric-à-brac, some antiques, handicrafts, clothes, plants, animals, books, furniture, household utensils… almost anything you can imagine could turn up here. You may be lucky enough to unearth some treasure, or you may find some curiosity you simply can't resist. Courteous bartering is acceptable in the street, but it's not so welcome in the stores. While strolling along the Ribera, the nearby river bank, don't forget to look in at some of the antique galleries: Nuevas Galerías (no. 12), Galerías Ribera (no. 15), Galerías Piquer (no. 29).

## Mercado de la Paz (57)
### Ayala 28, 28001 ☎ (91) 435 07 43

Ⓜ *Serrano* **Food** 🕐 *Mon.–Sat. 9–3pm, 5–8.30pm* ▭

In this remarkably well-organized food market selling some exceptional quality produce, you can choose a tasty souvenir from among Spain's finest and best-known gourmet delights: serrano or jabugo ham, chorizo, *lomo*, rustic cheeses, olives, fresh vegetables and fruits, or just feast your eyes and senses on the riches of this prosperous agricultural land.

57

56

58

food and second-hand books are also worth a detour. An opportunity to pick up a bargain, or waste a few pesetas.

## Cuesta de Moyano (58)
**Cuesta de Claudio Moyano, 28014**

Ⓜ *Atocha* **Second-hand books** 🕐 *nearly all the stalls are open during the week; on Sundays you have to get there between about 9.30am and 2pm*

The pretty wooden stalls along the Cuesta de Moyano have recently been renovated. Shaded by the awnings and the tall trees of the botanical gardens ➡ 98, you may find rare, second-hand books, as well as new ones at bargain prices. The book market marks the beginning of one the Madrileños' favorite walks, leading to Parque del Retiro ➡ 98.

## Not forgetting

▦ **Mercado de Sellos y Monedas (59)** Plaza Mayor, 28012
🕐 Sun., public holidays mornings
*Stamp and coin market where collectors, dealers and curious onlookers gather under the arcades of Plaza Mayor ➡ 92.*
▦ **Centro de Anticuarios de Lagasca (60)** Lagasca 36, 28001
*Antique dealers are scattered all over the Salamanca neighborhood. Some of the best ones, but also the most expensive, operate from this center.*

# Finding your way

## Location of the city
*Latitude N. 40° 24' - Longitude W. 3° 42'*
Madrid is at the heart of the Iberian
Peninsula, 400 miles from Barcelona
and 350 miles from Seville. At 2120
feet above sea level, it is also Europe's
highest capital.

## City layout
Madrid is divided into 21 *Distritos Municipales*,
numbered from the center outward: 01
(Centro), 02 (Arguanzela), 03 (Retiro) etc.
Prefixed by the figure 280, the number
determines the city code. Beware: this is not
the same as a zip code (also prefixed by 280).

# 6 Maps

## Mini street glossary

**Avenida**: avenue
**Calle**: street
**Callejón**: alley, cul-de-sac
**Camino**: way
**Carretera**: road
**Costanilla**: sloping alley
**Cuesta**: sloping street

**Glorieta**: traffic circle
**Pasaje**: passage
**Paseo**: boulevard
**Plaza**: square
**Puerta**: gate
**Ronda**: ring road
**Travesía**: way, passage

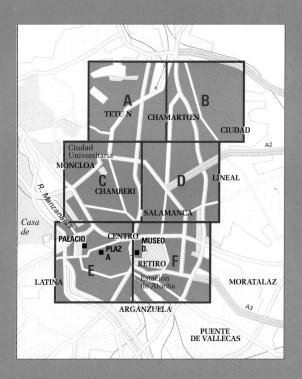

## Street index

Each street name is followed by a bold letter indicating which map to refer to, and a grid reference.

# Index

## Abbreviations

| | | | | | |
|---|---|---|---|---|---|
| *Av.* | = Avenida | *Glr.* | = Glorieta | *Pl.* | = Plaza |
| *C.* | = Calle | *M.* | = Metro | *Po.* | = Paseo |

# Subway map

**9** Herrera Oria

Fuencar|

Begoña

Barrio del Pilar

Chamartí|

Ventilla

Valdeacederas

**1** Plaza de Castilla

Tetuán

Estrecho

Cuzco

Alvarado

Lima

Guzmán el Bueno

**2** Cuatro Caminos

**8** Nuevos Ministerios

Repú|
Arge|

Metropolitano

**6**

Ríos Rosas

Ciudad Universitaria

Quevedo

Iglesia

Avda. Amér|

**3** Moncloa

San Bernardo

Rubén Darío

**4** Argüelles

Bilbao

de

Ventura Rodríguez

**10**

Noviciado

Colón

S|

Plaza de España

Tribunal

A. Martínez

Ve

**R** Príncipe Pío

Santo Domingo

Chueca

Gran Vía

p|
de V|

Lago

Puerta del Angel

Callao

Batán

Alto de Extremadura

**R** Opera

Sol

La Latina

Sevilla

Banco de Esp|

Tirso de Mol|

Antón M|

Puerta de Toledo

Lavapiés

Ato

Lucero

**6**

Acacias

Embajadores

Campamento

Laguna

Pirámides

Palos de la Frontera

Empalme

Carpetana

Marqués de Vadillo

Urgel

Delicias

**10** **5** Aluche

**P**

Oporto

**6**

Carabanchel

Vista Alegre

Opañel

Plaza Elíptica

Usera

Legazpi **3**

**8**

⟲ ⇌

Duque de Pastrana

Pío XII

**Esperanza** **4**

Colombia

Arturo Soria

Concha
Espina

Avda. de la Paz

Cruz del
Rayo

Alfonso XIII

Prosperidad

Cartagena

Parque de las
Avenidas

**7**

Barrio de la
Concepción

Diego de
León **Ventas** **2**

Lista

El Carmen  Quintana

Manuel
Becerra

Goya

O'Donnell

Ibiza

Retiro

Sainz de Baranda

Estrella

**6**

Vinateros

Artilleros

cha Renfe
⟲ ⇌

Conde de Casal

Menéndez
Pelayo

Pacífico

Puente de Vallecas

Nueva Numancia

Méndez
lvaro ⟲

Portazgo

Buenos Aires

Alto del Arenal

**Miguel Hernández** **1** P

**P** **5** **Canillejas**

Torre Arias

Suanzes

Ciudad Lineal

**Las Musas** **7**

Pueblo Nuevo

Ascao

García
Noblejas

Simancas

San Blas

**Pavones** **9**

◄ **Metro** ►

**Opening hours from
6am to l.30am**

⟲  Connection to suburban trains

⇌  Connection to RENFE trains

P  Parking

## General index

See pages 6–15 for practical information about getting there, getting around, and getting by.

# Index

We would like to thank the *Spanish Tourist Office* (OET), *Javier Calbet* of Acento Editorial, and all the organizations listed in the guide for their cooperation.

## Picture
# Credits

**1** and cover illustration Donald Grant
**6** Vincent de Lapomarède
**8** Kristof Chemineau (Airport map), Vincent de Lapomarède
**9** Hotel Sofitel
**10** RENFE (station exteriors, parking lot and trains), OET (station interior)
**12** Vincent de Lapomarède (subway and bus), Gallimard-Éric Guillemot (subway tickets)
**14** Gallimard-Éric Guillemot (money and newspapers)
**15** Gallimard-Éric Guillemot (phonecards)
**16** Vimagen Fotografos S.L.
**19** 1 Ritz, 2 Palace, 4 Tryp Reina Victoria
**21** 7 Arosa, 8 Gaudí, 9 Imaginaria, 10 Tryp Ambassador
**23** 13 NH Santo Mauro, 14 NH Embajada, 15 Tryp Fenix, 16 NH Sanvy
**25** 17 Villa Magna, 18 Wellington
**27** 22 Guy Saint Clair, 24 Vimagen Fotografos S.L., 25 NH Parque de las Avenidas, 27 NH Príncipe de Vergara
**29** 29 Vincent de Lapomarède, 30 Fernando Gordillo, 32 Style Escultor
**31** 34 Meliá Castilla, 37 Lola Heras, 39 Cuzco (caretaker), 39 Vincent de Lapomarède (drawings)
**33** 41 La Residencia de El Viso, 42 Aristos
**34** Pedro Larumbe-Juan A. Sancho

**37** 1 Casa Lucio, 2 Caroline Cuny, 4 De la Riva
**39** 5 Botín, 7 La Esquina del Real, 10 La Bola, 11 Cornucopia
**41** 12 Viridiana, 14 Errota -Zar, 16 Goya, 17 La Vaca Verónica
**43** 18 San Carlo, 19 Nicolás, 20 La Gamella
**45** 24 Ciao Madrid, 26 Al Mounia, 28 Pelotari
**47** 29 El Amparo, 30 La Paloma, 31 Teatriz, 32 La Trainera, 33 El Fogón
**49** 35 Gargantuel, 36 Castello 9, 37 El Pescador
**51** 39 Pedro Larumbe-Juan A. Sancho, 40 Berceo
**53** 43 El Bodegón, 44 Belagua, 45 Fdo. Sacristan
**55** 47 Las Batuecas, 49 Ana Fernandez
**57** 50 O'Pazo, 51 Goizeko Kabi, 55 Alboran
**59** 57 Casa Benigna, 58 La Atalaya
**61** 59 El Comité, 60 La Tahona, 62 El Cenachero
**63** 64 Casa d'a Troya, 65 La Misión, 66 Nicomedes
**65** 69 Aldaba, 70 (exterior) and 72 Vincent de Lapomarède, 70 Cabo Mayor (interior), 71 Vimagen Fotografos S.L.
**66** Joy
**69** 2 Castellana 99, 3 Vincent de Lapomarède, 4 Cafe de Oriente, 5 El Espejo
**71** 7 Handicap, 8 and badge

**73** 12 Cock, 13 Julio Moya, 16 Castellana 8
**75** 17 Auditorio Nacional de Música, 18 Fondation Juan March
**77** 19 Teatro de Bellas Artes, 21 Caroline Cuny, 22 Teatro Español, 23 Chicho (auditorium), 23 Vincent de Lapomarède (exterior), 23 Alberto Corazón (poster)
**79** 25 Teatro de la Zarzuela, 27 and 28 Vincent de Lapomarède
**81** 29 Gallimard-Éric Guillemot (plate), 29 Corral de la Morería (dancers), 30 Vincent de Lapomarède, castanets Hotel Villa Magna
**83** 34 Gallimard-Éric Guillemot, 35 Florida Park, 36 Vincent de Lapomarède, 37 Scala Melia
**85** 39 Joy, 41 Dusko Despotovic, 43 Palacio de Gaviria
**87** 44 Subway, 46 and 47 Vincent de Lapomarède
**88** OET
**91** 1 (door) and 3 Caroline Cuny, 1 (façade, dining room) and 2 OET
**93** OET
**95** 9 (Baroque door) and 12 Caroline Cuny, 9 OET (Metropolis building)
**97** 13 Museo del Prado, 14 Museo Thyssen-Bornemisza, 19 Museo del Ejército
**99** 20 (building), 21 (lake) and 22 OET, 20 Centro Cultural Reina Sofia (interior), 21 (Palacio de Cristal) and 23 Caroline Cuny
**101** 26 Javier Calbet (façade), 26 OET (bullring), 26 J. M. Navia (torero and picador)
**103** 28 Museo de América,

30 OET, 32 Caroline Cuny
**105** 33 OET, 34 Archivo Fotográfico Museo Arqueológico Nacional, 35 Museo Municipal, 37 Vincent de Lapomarède
**107** plaques, 40 and 41 (panoramic view) Caroline Cuny, 41 Vincent de Lapomarède (sculpture)
**109** 42 and 43 OET, 44 Caroline Cuny, 45 Palacio de Congresos
**110-123** OET
**124** Gallimard-Javier Calbet
**127** 2 Monsy, 4 Seseña, 6 Javier Sanz
**129** 7 Casa Jiménez, 8 and 10 Gallimard-Éric Guillemot, 9 and 11 Vincent de Lapomarède, 13 J. Jorge
**131** 14 El Corte Inglés, 16 Pedro Larumbe (façade), 16 (flags), 16 (street) and 17 Caroline Cuny
**133** 19 Casa del Libro, 21 Grassy
**135** 24 Antigua Casa Talavera, 25 Hernández, 28 Gallimard-Javier Calbet
**137** 31 Piamonte, 32 Joaquín Berao, 33 Patrimonio Comunal Olivarero, 35 Excrupulus Net, 36 Almirante 23
**139** 38 Farrutx, 40 Lœwe, 42 Roberto Verino
**141** 46 ABB Fotografos, 47 El Caballo, 48 Santa
**143** 52 Coronel Tapioca, 53 Moda Shopping, 54 Estudio San Simon, 55 Alexandra Bellinger
**145** 56 (bags), 56 (birds), 57 and 58 Caroline Cuny, 56 Vincent de Lapomarède (umbrella and bric-à-brac)
**146** Alfonso Vargas García